GOD BLESS THE VOLS

ED McMINN

Devotions for
the Die-Hard
Tennessee Fan

GOD
BLESS
THE
VOLS

HOWARD BOOKS
A DIVISION OF SIMON & SCHUSTER
New York   London   Toronto   Sydney

Our purpose at Howard Books is to:
• *Increase faith* in the hearts of growing Christians
• *Inspire holiness* in the lives of believers
• *Instill hope* in the hearts of struggling people everywhere
Because He's coming again!

 Howard Books, a division of Simon & Schuster, Inc.
HOWARD 1230 Avenue of the Americas, New York, NY 10020
BOOKS

God Bless the Vols © 2007 Ed McMinn

Agent: Les Stobbe

Library of Congress Cataloging-in-Publication Data

ISBN-13: 978-1-4165-4189-9

ISBN-13: 978-1-58229-638-8

10 9 8 7 6 5 4 3 2 1

HOWARD colophon is a registered trademark of Simon & Schuster, Inc.

Manufactured in the United States of America

For information regarding special discounts for bulk purchases,
please contact Simon & Schuster Special Sales at 1-800-456-6798 or
business@simonandschuster.com.

Edited by Between the Lines
Cover design by John Lucas
Interior design by Jaime Putorti

Scripture quotations are taken from the New Revised Standard Version Bible.
Copyright © 1989 by the Division of Christian Education of the National Council
of the Churches of Christ in the United States of America. All rights reserved.

To Grace Church,
Faithful volunteers for Jesus Christ

CONTENTS

GOD
BLESS
THE
VOLS

In the Beginning

Read Genesis 1, 2:1–3.

"God saw everything that he had made, and indeed, it was very good" (v. 1:31).

Sack races, wheelbarrow races, and high kicks rather than football and basketball. Suspenders and shaving mugs rather than championship rings. In the beginning that was athletics at the University of Tennessee.

The driving force behind the first athletic contests at UT was a pair of professors. According to Russ Bebb in *The Big Orange,* in the late 1880s Charles Plumb and Charles Summers organized the first intramural field days at Tennessee. In January 1889 the events included "a potato race, sack race, fifty-yard dash, high kick contest, and standing long jump" plus a wheelbarrow race. The last event was the highlight of the day because there were several wrecks, some precipitated by Professor Summers himself, who insisted on racing.

In the spring of that same year, Bebb said, Professor Plumb was at it again, organizing a field day that included prizes for the winners. The athlete with the greatest number of points for the day won a silver shaving mug and a silver-handled brush.

Other prizes included a gold-headed cane, a pair of suspenders (satin, no less), a set of Charles Dickens's novels, and a straw hat.

In the beginning, this was the athletic program at the University of Tennessee.

Beginnings are important, but what we make of them—what follows—is even more important. Every morning, you get an important gift from God: a new beginning. The day lies before you expectant and pristine. You can use it to pay a debt, start a new relationship, replace a burned-out light bulb, tell your family you love them, chase a dream, solve a nagging problem, right old wrongs . . . or not.

God simply provides the gift. How you use it is up to you. People often talk wistfully about starting over or making a new beginning. God gives you the chance with the dawning of every new day.

The most important key to achieving great success is to decide upon your goal and launch, get started, take action, move.
—BASKETBALL COACH JOHN WOODEN

➤ **Every day is not just a dawn; it is a precious chance to start over or begin anew.**

What a Day!

Read Proverbs 6:12–23.

"A scoundrel and a villain goes around with crooked speech, winking the eyes, shuffling the feet, pointing the fingers, with perverted mind devising evil, continually sowing discord" (vv. 12–14).

His success was so astounding it defies belief, but something besides ability, hard work, and luck played a key role in his career.

Chuck Rohe was the head track coach at Tennessee from 1963 to 1971. In *Tales of the Tennessee Vols,* Marvin West said that the legendary coach's "run from a sub-zero start in 1962 to seven consecutive SEC championships is one of the genuine sports miracles of the past century." Tennessee was so dominant that the Orangemen single-handedly "raised the level of performance throughout the South" as other schools scrambled to keep from getting embarrassed by the Volunteer juggernaut.

Part of Rohe's success certainly can be attributed to the talent he lured to Knoxville. He doubled as the coordinator of football recruiting, and he purposefully sought out athletes who were gifted enough to play football and run track. But Rohe had a secret that went beyond mere coaching skill, athletic ability, and hustle. He had a great attitude.

His outlook was always positive, even "super-positive" as West put it. West said that even if nature was brewing up one of her worst storms, Rohe "would meet distance runners for cross-country training at six a.m. with this trademark greeting: 'What a day!'"

How's your attitude? You can fuss because your house is not as big as some, because a coworker talks too much, or because you have to take pills every day. Or you can appreciate your home for providing warmth and shelter, the coworker for the lively conversation, and the medicine for keeping you at least reasonably healthy. The difference is not facts but attitude.

Life can be either endured or enjoyed, suffered or celebrated. The difference lies largely in your attitude. Good or bad, the one you adopt goes a long way toward determining the quality of your life.

I became an optimist when I discovered that I wasn't going to win any more games by being anything else.
—EARL WEAVER

▶ **Your attitude determines more than your mood; it shapes the kind of person you are.**

Good as One's Word

Read Matthew 12:33–37.

"Out of the abundance of the heart the mouth speaks. The good person brings good things out of a good treasure, and the evil person brings evil things out of an evil treasure" (vv. 34–35).

"**D**on't worry about that, son."

What? Don't worry about it! He had just missed a game-tying extra point late in the Cotton Bowl!

But that's what General Bob Neyland told his dejected kicker as he trotted to the sidelines. Remember this was the man of whom Volunteer all-American Beattie Feathers told Bob Gilbert in *Neyland,* "Nobody ever wanted to win a football game more than the General."

Fourth-ranked Tennessee met third-ranked Texas in the 1951 Cotton Bowl. The Longhorns led 14–7 when the Vols drove eighty-three yards early in the fourth quarter for a touchdown, but then the extra point went awry. Tennessee trailed 14–13. Pat Shires, the tailback who missed the kick, told Gilbert, "Neyland met me coming off the field and said, 'Don't worry about that, son. We didn't come here to tie.'"

Certainly frustrated by the crucial miscue, the legendary coach could well have excoriated his kicker, but instead he chose to offer encouragement and support. He offered good words when a lesser person might have chosen evil ones.

These days, everybody's got something to say and a place to say it. Talk radio. Twenty-four-hour sports and news TV channels. *Oprah*. *The View*. Talk has really become cheap.

But words still have power, and that includes not just those of the talking heads and pundits on television, but you also. Your words are perhaps the most powerful force you possess for good or for bad. The words you speak today can belittle, wound, humiliate, and destroy. They can also inspire, heal, protect, and create.

Your every word is important; others are always listening to and being affected by them.

And that missed extra point Shires wasn't to worry about? As usual, the General was right; it didn't matter. Late in the game, fullback Andy Kozar scored from the one and Tennessee won 20–14.

My dad has always taught me these words: care and share.
—Tiger Woods

▶ **Choose your words carefully; they are the most powerful force you have for good or for bad.**

Homework

Read Joshua 1:1–9.

*"This book of the law shall not depart out of your mouth;
you shall meditate on it day and night, so that you may
be careful to act in accordance with all that is written in it.
For then you shall make your way prosperous, and then
you shall be successful" (v. 8).*

The on-court exploits of the 1997–98 Lady Volunteers basketball team are now the stuff of legend. It was arguably the
greatest women's basketball team ever, finishing at 39–0 and
winning the national championship, UT's third straight. The
team beat its opponents by an average of thirty points a game.

But the young women who made up that team were also ul-
trasuccessful off the court and in the classroom. In *Raise the
Roof,* Pat Summitt said that the semester after the team finished its sensational championship run, "The Lady Vols turned
in one of the best classroom performances I had ever seen in
our program." More than half of the team had a 3.0 grade-
point average or higher; "the rest were close."

The devotion to academics was as intense—well, almost—
as the devotion to basketball. During the season when a player

skipped class, Summitt called the team together and threatened to stick the whole bunch in a study hall if any member of the team cut class again. "One more of these and you're all in study hall twelve hours a week," she declared.

For Pat Summitt and the Lady Volunteers, homework meant studying and preparing not just for basketball but also for class work and for life.

Are you studying and preparing so none of life's challenges or surprises will lay you low? Life requires assembly, much like your kids' bicycles. You know the drill; even with parts scattered all around you, you work undismayed because you can read the instructions.

Life, too, has an instruction book so you can get it right. It's probably by your bed or on a living room table. It's the Bible, given to you by God so you can get through life in good shape by reading the instructions. You can study and prepare; you can do your homework.

It's not the will to win, but the will to prepare to win that makes the difference.
—BEAR BRYANT

> **You have readily available a set of instructions on how to assemble your life: the Bible.**

A Change of Plans

Read Genesis 18:20–33.

"The LORD said, 'If I find at Sodom fifty righteous in the city, I will forgive the whole place for their sake'" (v. 26).

With the game on the line in the closing seconds, a good basketball coach always has a plan. The Volunteers had one for the last shot in overtime of the second round of the 1981 NCAA Tournament—and it didn't work. Thank goodness!

Don DeVoe's team finished the regular season 20-7 and ranked fifteenth. After a first-round bye, the Vols ran into a hot Virginia Commonwealth team that had won sixteen straight. Regulation ended in a 56–56 tie. In the era before the shot clock, the Rams held the ball for one shot to win.

But the Vols forced a turnover and held the ball themselves. As Randy Moore told it in *Hoop Tales: Tennessee Volunteers Men's Basketball,* DeVoe called time-out with nineteen seconds left. Dale Ellis, one of the greatest players in Tennessee history, recalled that DeVoe wanted Howard Wood to take the last shot. "The ball was supposed to come to me, and I was supposed to pass it to Howard in the corner," Ellis said.

When Ellis got the ball, though, he saw that Wood was covered. So Ellis let loose with a sixteen-footer that caught nothing but net just as the buzzer sounded. The Vols had a win!

We all change our plans sometimes—even God. But what could possibly make the God of the universe change his mind? Prayer. Someone—maybe you—talks to God, who not only listens but also considers what is being asked of him.

You may feel uncomfortable praying. Maybe you're reluctant and embarrassed; perhaps you feel you're not very good at it. But nobody majors in prayer at school, and as for being reluctant, what have you got to lose? Your answer may even be a change of plans on God's part. Such is the power of prayer.

There are two things you can do with your head down:
play golf and pray.

—LEE TREVINO

➤ **Prayer is powerful; it may even change God's mind.**

The Eye of a Needle

Read Matthew 19:23–26.

"It is easier for a camel to go through the eye of a needle than for someone who is rich to enter the kingdom of God" (v. 24).

The goal posts must have looked about as wide as the eye of a needle to Sammy Burklow in the 1957 Gator Bowl against Texas A&M. Here he was being called on in the closing minutes to win the game when he had never successfully kicked a field goal before.

Coach Bowden Wyatt was encouraging. According to Russ Bebb in *The Big Orange,* Wyatt gave Burklow a pat on the backside and told him to break the 0–0 tie with only five minutes left in the game by saying, "Son, go in there and kick it. It's just like an extra point."

That it was. The ball was less than a yard from the goal line, squarely in the center of the field, and Burklow was 15 of 17 for the season on extra points. But he was 0 for 2 in his career on field-goal attempts and had not even tried a single one that year.

So with the pressure of time running out and with his lack

of experience, the goal posts must have narrowed to the width of that needle's eye as Burklow lined up for the kick. Even if it were "just like an extra point," the kick was not a given.

But Burklow nailed it—and Tennessee had a 3–0 win.

Are you rich? Even if you're struggling to keep the bills current and putting off buying that fishing boat, the answer is probably yes. Compared with much of the world, most of us are wealthy indeed.

So did Jesus really say that because you've got a few dollars in the bank, the doors of heaven will slam shut in your face? No. But he served notice that you must place nothing in your life ahead of God. Not even a new car or a pool table. In God alone—not in the riches and luxuries of this world—must you trust.

> *Money can buy you everything but happiness.*
> *It can pay your fare to everywhere but heaven.*
> —PETE MARAVICH

➤ **No riches or luxuries must come before God in your life.**

The Jesus Way

Read Romans 13:8–14.

"The night is far gone, the day is near. Let us then lay aside the works of darkness and put on the armor of light" *(v. 12).*

Was General Bob Neyland, who coached at Tennessee from 1926 to 1934, 1936 to 1940, and 1946 to 1952, the greatest college football coach ever? The record says so.

In 1990 Bob Gilbert declared in *Neyland: The Gridiron General* that of all the head coaches at major colleges with twenty years or more on the job, Neyland's won-lost record (173-31-12 and a winning percentage of 82.9) was the best.

The Neyland way of doing things was a very particular way. His single-wing offense was cited by one sports editor as "an accurate reflection of Neyland—tough, common-sense, and planned with the skill of a symphony score."

With such a unique and successful system, Neyland naturally had his disciples, and Tennessee naturally called upon them when the general officially retired from coaching after the 1953 Cotton Bowl, remaining as UT's athletics director. Assistant coach Harvey Robinson was hand-picked by Neyland to succeed him. After the 1954 season Neyland fired Robinson and hired another disciple and former player, Bowden Wyatt. Tennessee experienced another changing of the guard in 1963. Another Neyland disciple, Bob Woodruff, had been hired as athletics director that year; his choice for the next head coach was a man he had coached at Florida and thus initiated into Neyland's philosophy: Doug Dickey.

All these men were expected to coach and to comport themselves a certain way: the Neyland way.

Even more important is following another way: the Jesus way. His way is to live and to act with love at all times. It's basically simple, even if it is downright daunting. You act toward others in a way that would not embarrass you were your day to be broadcast on CNN. You think about others in a way that would not humiliate you should your thoughts be the plotline for a new CBS sitcom.

Make your actions and thoughts those of love: at all times, in all things, toward all people. It's the Jesus way.

That's the thing about sports. Once people can play together, they see they can live together.
—LEGENDARY GRAMBLING COACH EDDIE ROBINSON

≫ **To follow Jesus is to act with love at all times, in all things, and toward all people.**

Making a Joyful Noise

Read Psalm 66.

"Make a joyful noise to God, all the earth" (v. 1).

When more than a hundred thousand of your closest friends stand up and cheer at the same time, the noise is awesome and intimidating. That's what happens in the fall at Neyland Stadium.

In *Neyland: Life of a Stadium,* Barry Parker and Robin Hood described the sound: "As 'Rocky Top' is played and the band forms the Power 'T,' one hundred-thousand-plus roar as one— a sound that doesn't build as it would in a smaller, open stadium, but ignites in the bowl with percussive force."

And that's only the beginning. "Salvos of screams and cheers burst in the air. 'Yeaaahhh!' goes the crowd. . . . As Tennessee drives, emotions build. Stomping their feet in unison, fans produce a tremor in the stands. . . . Cheerleaders bark through megaphones, . . . sound and energy mount in swells. . . . A score ignites a thunderous roar and a crackle of fireworks."

Such awesome and intimidating noise is expected from the UT faithful. After all, how can Tennessee fans possibly sit on their hands and not make a joyful noise when the Volunteers score? We expect each other to shout and jump and generally act with gleeful abandon.

Perhaps there are times other than a UT game when you've acted not quite like the sane, reserved, and responsible person you really are. The birth of your first child. Your wedding day. The concert of your favorite band. The fishing trip when you caught that big ol' bass. You whooped it up pretty good.

But what about making a powerful racket to God in celebration of his love for you? God doesn't necessarily require that you walk around waving pompoms and shouting, "Yay, God!" A nice little "thank you" is sufficient when it's sincerely delivered. To God, that is a joyful noise.

Southern football fans are knowledgeable, fair—and loud.
—UT BROADCASTER GEORGE MOONEY

➤ **For God, a joyful noise is a heartfelt "thank you," even when it's whispered.**

A Second Chance

Read John 7:53–8:11.

"Jesus said, 'Neither do I condemn you. Go your way, and from now on do not sin again'" (v. 8:11).

Volunteer guard Michael Brooks was looking for a second chance.

Brooks, a junior, hoped to get that second chance in the 1983 NCAA Tournament. In *Hoop Tales: Tennessee Volunteers Men's Basketball,* Randy Moore wrote, "Brooks, whose missed free throws had contributed to Tennessee's NCAA ouster the previous year, hoped for a chance to atone."

Led by Dale Ellis, the Vols of 1981–82 finished the regular season 18-8, tied for first in the SEC. They whipped Southwest Louisiana in the opening round of the NCAA Tournament.

In the second-round game, the Vols missed four of five free throws in the last 3:12 of the game. Moore noted, "Three of the misfires—including one by Brooks—came on the front end of one-and-ones, and those six potential points proved decisive as the Big Orange bowed 54–51" to Virginia.

Brooks had led the effort with twenty-four points, but still he sought atonement the following year. And he got it. Against

Marquette in the opening round, the game was tied with sixty-one seconds left when Brooks was fouled. He sank both free throws. Then, with UT leading only 55–54 with five seconds to play, he sank two more free throws to lock up the 57–56 win.

Second chances. Mulligans. It's a shame life doesn't emulate golf and give us a do-over now and then. If you could go back and repair that relationship that meant so much to you, wouldn't you? If you got a second chance to take that job you passed up, wouldn't you? If you got another try at going out with that dream date, wouldn't you?

God is a God of second chances—and third chances and fourth chances. No matter how many mistakes you make—and we all make a bunch—God will never give up on you.

Things could be worse. Suppose your errors were counted and published every day, like those of a baseball player.
—Source unknown

▷ **Even though you keep making mistakes, God never gives up on you.**

Home Improvement

Read 1 Corinthians 6:12–20.

"Do you not know that your body is a temple of the Holy Spirit within you . . . ? For you were bought with a price; therefore glorify God in your body" (vv. 19–20).

A home of any sort is better than being homeless, but once a home is found, we often seek ways to make it better. Neyland Stadium, dedicated in 1921 as Shields-Watkins Field, was a dream come true for players and fans accustomed to playing Tennessee's home games at Wait Field, a place with rocks and hard ground and only a few wooden benches.

Quickly, though, the little stadium's shortcomings became apparent. In *Neyland: Life of a Stadium,* Barry Parker and Robin Hood quoted the campus newspaper in 1925 as saying, "Making a field of Shields-Watkins will, if nothing more, reduce the athletic department's laundry bill." Scoffed the student writer, "Fans are tired of seeing Tennessee's wonderful football teams play in a sea of mud." The field's flat surface meant poor—if any—drainage, and rain quickly turned the field into a quagmire.

So before the 1926 season, the playing surface was sloped

and sodded, creating the traditional turtleback shape so water could run off the field into catch basins. To protect the field from too much wear and tear, a practice field was marked off adjacent to the stadium. On the east side seventeen rows with thirty-six hundred pine seats and locker rooms underneath were constructed.

Those improvements were made in a stadium barely five years old because the structure needed to be better. Subsequent repairs and expansions were made for the same reason. Great as it is, Neyland Stadium will always be subject to renovation to make it better.

The same is true for our lives; they can always stand some improvement. It's not just physical changes, though, that are necessary; you need to care for yourself spiritually, too. Keep your body and your soul in shape. You are always "under construction" as far as God is concerned, because you can always get better.

The principle is competing against yourself.
It's about self-improvement, about being better
than you were the day before.
—NFL QUARTERBACK STEVE YOUNG

> **Renovation and sprucing up should be ongoing for your body and soul.**

God's Workforce

Read John 15:12–17.

"I chose you. And I appointed you to go and bear fruit, fruit that will last" (v. 16).

"**A** man can live without love but not without work."

According to Russ Bebb in *The Big Orange,* that was one of General Bob Neyland's favorite sayings. Neyland particularly lived by this motto as the 1938 season got under way, and he demanded the same of his assistant coaches and his players. What primarily inspired the hard work was the 1937 season, when Tennessee lost to Alabama, Auburn, and Vanderbilt. "I'll never lose three games in one season again," Neyland vowed to some of his players.

The off-season lasted only thirty-five days. The Vols buried Ole Miss 32–0 on December 4 and then started practice on January 9. Bebb wrote that Neyland met his assistants at the office every morning at six, and spring drills lasted into April.

The practices were no picnics either. According to Bebb, five players suffered broken bones in the spring. When "Hodges (Burr) West went down with a broken leg, Neyland, standing over him, shouted, 'If you hadn't been loafing you wouldn't have hurt it.'"

This was not a time for the player or coach who shunned hard work. Neyland set the example in his determination to put the Vols back on top.

How do you feel about hard work? Do you embrace it or try to avoid it? No matter how hard you may try, you really can't escape hard work. Funny thing about all these labor-saving devices like cell phones and laptop computers: You're probably working longer and harder than ever. Even retirees are working more these days. For many of us, our work defines us perhaps more than any other aspect of our lives. But there's a workforce you're part of that doesn't show up in any Labor Department statistics or IRS records.

You're part of God's staff. You are charged with the awesome responsibility of spreading his love around as freely as possible. The hours are awful—24/7—but the benefits are out of this world.

I've always believed that if you put in the work, the results will come.
—MICHAEL JORDAN

▶ **God has a job for you: spreading his love.**

One Tough Cookie

Read 2 Corinthians 11:21–29.

"Besides other things, I am under daily pressure because of my anxiety for all the churches" (v. 28).

"A drill sergeant in sneakers . . . a lipstick-wearing pit bull."

That's what players encountered in 1974 when they met Pat Summitt, the new women's basketball coach at Tennessee, according to Randy Moore in *Hoop Tales: Tennessee Lady Volunteers.* Moore said Summitt's approach was "you can start out tough and let up, but if you start out soft you may never get the results you need."

Any mellowing on Summitt's part over the years was only relative, however, as two incidents Moore related illustrate. In 1980 the Lady Vols arrived home early in the morning after collapsing in the last half against South Carolina. Summitt ordered them—still wearing their sweaty uniforms—onto the practice floor to play the half they hadn't played earlier. Later in the 1980s, Summitt heard team members had partied all night the evening before. In response, she placed garbage cans at each corner of the gym and ran the players until they vomited into them.

Perhaps the most legendary story of Summitt's toughness involved her refusal to allow the plane she was on to land in Virginia so she could give birth to her son, even though her water had broken. Virginia's Lady Cavaliers had upset Tennessee the season before in the NCAA tournament, so she didn't want her son born in Virginia.

You don't have to be a legendary coach to be tough. Going to work every morning, sticking by your rules for the children, making hard decisions about your aging parents' care—you've got to be tough every day just to live honorably, decently, and justly.

Living faithfully requires toughness, too, though in America chances are you won't be imprisoned, stoned, or flogged this week for your faith as Paul was. Still, society and popular culture exert subtle, psychological, daily pressures on you to turn your back on your faith and your values.

Hang tough. Keep the faith.

Winning isn't imperative, but getting tougher
in the fourth quarter is.
—BEAR BRYANT

> *Life demands more than mere physical toughness;*
> *you must be spiritually tough too.*

Bad Times—Good Witness

Read Philippians 1:3–14.

"What has happened to me has actually helped to spread the gospel, . . . and most of the brothers and sisters, having been made confident in the LORD by my imprisonment, dare to speak the word with greater boldness and without fear" (vv. 12, 14).

David Moss never really got his chance at Tennessee.

He could have been a star. As Marvin West put it in *Tales of the Tennessee Vols,* Moss "didn't have a great shooting touch when he came out of Ringgold, Georgia, but he brought a great attitude and a wonderful set of legs." His legs were so good, he was Georgia's state high-jump champion in 1974.

The future looked bright for Moss when he lettered his freshman year. He was a projected starter his sophomore season.

And then cancer got in the way. He had a leg amputated at the hip. West pointed out that the surgery "was a horrible disaster for an athlete, but not quite enough to wipe the smile from [Moss's] face."

With basketball and UT in his blood, Moss did what he

could, helping out around the offices, helping coach the freshmen, and working toward his degree. But the cancer came back.

Moss made it to Senior Night 1977, the last game of the season. West declared he received the "loudest and longest" ovation of the night. A pretty fair ballplayer named Ernie Grunfeld was second. Moss's illness and subsequent death became his greatest triumph. Coach Ray Mears said that, in facing death, David Moss "taught us all something about living."

Loved ones die. You're downsized. Your biopsy indicates cancer. Your spouse could be having an affair. Hard, tragic times are as much a part of life as breath. How do you handle them? You can buckle to your knees in despair and cry, "Why me?" Or you can hit your knees in prayer and ask, "What do I do with this?"

Setbacks and tragedies are opportunities to reveal and to develop true character and abiding faith. Your faithfulness—not your skipping merrily along through life without pain—is what reveals the depth of your love for God.

If I were to say, "God, why me?" about the bad things, then I should have said, "God, why me?" about the good things that happened in my life.
—ARTHUR ASHE

▷ **Faithfulness to God requires faith even in—especially in—the hard times.**

The Ultimate Makeover

Read 2 Corinthians 5:11–21.

"If anyone is in Christ, there is a new creation: everything old has passed away; see, everything has become new!" (v. 17).

Was Ron Widby a great football player or a great basketball player for the University of Tennessee?

He was both, and in his senior year of 1966–67, he had what may be the greatest single season ever by a UT athlete.

In the fall Widby was a football player. He was all-American and the NCAA punting champion, averaging 43.8 yards on forty-eight punts. In the winter Widby made himself over into one of UT's best basketball players ever. That fabulous senior season he was named all-American and SEC Player of the Year. He averaged 22.1 points and 8.7 rebounds to lead a young Vol team to the SEC title.

That versatility made life hectic around Christmastime, when the football team prepared for a bowl game and the basketball team played in tournaments. For instance, as a senior Widby played in the Sugar Bowl basketball tournament in New Orleans on Thursday and Friday and punted in the Gator Bowl in Jacksonville, Florida, on Saturday.

It wasn't just two sports, either. The article "Ron Widby Led the Vols" declared Widby to be "the last four-sport letterman at Tennessee with three varsity letters in football, three in basketball, and one each in baseball and golf." He continually had to make himself over, reshaping his physical abilities and mental approaches as he changed the game he played.

Ever considered a makeover? TV shows have shown us how changes in clothes, hair, and makeup can radically alter the way a person looks. But these changes are only skin deep. Even with a makeover, the real you—the person inside—remains unchanged. How can you make over that part of you?

Jesus does that by introducing you to a new ideal: himself. When he makes you over, you realize that gaining Jesus's good opinion—not the world's—is all that really matters. And he isn't interested in how you look but in how you act.

> *Don't think that the way you are today*
> *is the way you'll always be.*
> —VINCE DOOLEY

> **Jesus is the ultimate makeover artist; he can make you over without changing the way you look.**

A Strategy for Success

Read Joshua 6:1–20.

"You shall march around the city . . . for six days. . . . On the seventh day you shall march around the city seven times, the priests blowing the trumpets. . . . Then all the people shall shout with a great shout; and the wall of the city will fall down" (vv. 3, 4, 5).

Legendary UT coach Bob Neyland was a master of mind games as well as football games.

In 1932 in Birmingham, the Vols trailed Alabama 3–0 at halftime as the teams played in a driving rainstorm. Surely Coach Neyland would take the wind to start the third quarter and help his struggling offense out. Everybody knew that one touchdown would win this thing.

But Neyland had another idea entirely, and it turned out he was two steps ahead of everybody. As Randy Moore wrote in *Stadium Stories: Tennessee Volunteers,* Neyland elected to give Alabama the wind in the third quarter. "They have a lead to protect," Neyland told his team at halftime, "and they'll have to be conservative, taking no chances on a sloppy field. We'll get the wind in the fourth quarter; we'll be able to strike, and they will be helpless to stop us or retaliate."

The coach's strategy worked just as he called it. Alabama was content to sit on its 3–0 lead in the third quarter. In the fourth quarter, though, Tennessee relentlessly used the wind to gain ground on each exchange of punts. Finally, Beattie Feathers scored for a 7–3 Volunteer win. Neyland's plan had worked to perfection.

Successful living takes planning. You go to school to improve your chances for a better-paying job. You use blueprints to build your home. You plan for retirement. You map out your vacation to have the best time. You even plan your children— sometimes. Much of your life is carefully planned.

Successful death takes planning too. That's why you buy life insurance. But God has the ultimate plan for death, and while our most careful arrangements sometimes get wrecked by such things as the economy and unexpected illness, God's plan for eternity is foolproof. Jesus is a sure thing.

If you don't know where you are going, you will wind up somewhere else.
—Yogi Berra

Success in life takes planning and strategy; success in death does too, and God has the plan for you.

Dreams That Don't Come True

Read John 14:18–27.

"Peace I leave with you; my peace I give to you" (v. 27).

Dreams don't always come true in sports. Such was the reality for the UT men's basketball team of 2000–2001 and senior point guard Tony Harris.

It was to be the greatest basketball season in Tennessee history, and Harris was to lead the way. Writing for CNNSI.com in "Forget Football," Carl Bialik said, "Tennessee fans are counting on [Harris] to lead the Vols to a national championship in, of all things, basketball." Preseason polls had the Volunteers ranked as high as number five. Harris told Bialik that fans came up to him on campus to say, "I know you're going to take us to the Final Four and win the championship."

Marvin West said in *Tales of the Tennessee Vols* that Harris was a preseason all-American pick. It was to be a very good year.

It wasn't. Harris suffered an ankle injury, and it affected his shooting. The team lost eleven games and fell to UNC-

Charlotte in the opening round of the NCAA Tournament. Harris didn't even make the all-SEC team, let alone all-American.

West said that after the UNC-Charlotte game, Harris "sat, still in uniform, in the shower until the dressing room cleared." The dream was gone.

Remember that million dollars you were going to make before you were thirty? That perfect love affair that would lead to an ideal marriage? The great American novel you were going to write?

Dreams get more difficult to hold on to the older you get. Surrendering your dreams is part of the emotional turmoil and distress you routinely face, and sometimes inner peace eludes you. But into the midst of all this anxiety comes Jesus, promising peace in the form of certainty about eternity, a calm amid the turmoil and havoc of the world's storms. It isn't just a dream; it's a promise.

> *If you ever dream of beating me,*
> *you better wake up and apologize.*
> —MUHAMMAD ALI

▷ *Jesus gives us something better than a dream; he gives us a promise.*

Cheers

Read Matthew 21:1–11.

"The crowds that went ahead of him and that followed were shouting" (v. 9).

Some of the first recorded cheers in Tennessee football history probably won't make a comeback anytime soon.

In his book *The Big Orange,* Russ Bebb described some UT yells that were popular in the early days of the game. Bebb said that a favorite cheer around the turn of the century was "U of T, rah, rah, rah, rah! U of T, rah, rah, rah, rah!"

The cheers were especially prevalent after the first-ever meeting between Tennessee and Georgia in 1899 in Knoxville. UT won 5–0, and the fans started a bonfire and sang and yelled all night long. They shouted, "Hur-rah, hur-rah! Tennessee, Tennessee! Rah, rah, rah!" They also shouted the night away with "Rah, rah, rah! Rah, rah, rah! Rah, rah, rah! Tennessee!" And then there is the ever-forgettable "U-T, rah! U-T, rah! U-T, Tiger! Sis, boom, bah!"

They may not have been very original, but they certainly were heartfelt and were delivered with great enthusiasm. In the case of the aforementioned Georgia game, they also were delivered with sixteen cannon shots, the rattle of musketry, and songs of victory from the women students.

Encouraging and supporting someone else through loud cries and cheers has surely been around as long as humans have. Imagine a Tennessee athletic event without any cheering!

Chances are you go to work every day, do your job well, and then go home to your family. This country couldn't run without you; you're indispensable to the nation's efficiency. Even so, nobody cheers for you or waves pompoms in your face. Your name probably will never elicit a standing ovation when a PA announcer calls it.

It's just as well. Public opinion is fickle. Adulation is fleeting. Just ask Jesus, who was the object of raucous cheering when he entered triumphantly into Jerusalem. Five days later the crowd screamed for his execution.

But you do have one personal cheerleader for sure: God.

A cheerleader is a dreamer that never gives up.
—Source unknown

▸ **You may not know it, but just like the sports stars, you have a cheerleader: God.**

The Good Old Days

Read Psalm 102.

"My days pass away like smoke. . . . But you are the same, and your years have no end" (vv. 3, 27).

Times change.

It's a brutal truth of life that time just never stands still. Sometimes that's a good thing. Time often can erase pain and traumatic memories. Frequently, though, time changes places and people for the worse, until they become nothing more than fond memories, nostalgia, a conscious yearning for good old days that may never have existed.

Nathan Dougherty, a member of the National Football Foundation's College Football Hall of Fame, was present at the beginning; he played when the first forward pass was thrown in a UT game. His association with the university carried him into the SEC and the modern age of college sports. He saw many changes.

According to Russ Bebb in *The Big Orange*, Dougherty was there in 1907 when George Levene came in as UT's first salaried football coach for the princely sum of $750 a season. Perhaps with a wistful note in his voice, Dougherty told Bebb,

"Over the years the conferences have taken athletics out of the hands of the students and put it in the hands of the faculty and then made the university itself responsible for the athletic program."

The "good old days" are gone forever, though. The game Dougherty played and the atmosphere in which he played no longer exist. Times change.

The current of your life sweeps you along until you realize you've lived long enough to have a past—and parts of it you remember fondly. The stunts you pulled with your high-school pals. Your first apartment. That dance with your first love. The special beach vacation (and only you know why it was special).

Good times, good memories—and in our uncertain world, you cling to the old, familiar ways for the stability they provide. The only anchor that really holds, though, is God. God is life's lone constant.

Times change; God doesn't.

A trophy carries dust. Memories last forever.
—MARY LOU RETTON

> *In our ever-changing and bewildering world, God is the only constant.*

Running for Your Life

Read John 20:1–10.

"Peter and the other disciple set out and went toward the tomb. The two were running together, but the other disciple outran Peter and reached the tomb first" (vv. 3–4).

Richmond Flowers was used to outrunning defensive backs, but in the summer of 1967, one of Tennessee's greatest receivers ever was up against a new opponent: a horse.

In *Tales of the Tennessee Vols,* Marvin West said Volunteer quarterback Dewey Warren dreamed up the best-of-three forty-yard races between Tennessee's fastest football player and Tellico Plains's fastest quarter horse as a daily feature of a three-day rodeo. Thanks to a promotional campaign, the crowd "lined up twenty deep for the first night," according to Dewey. Flowers, meanwhile, was a little concerned. "People kept talking until it got to be a really big deal," he said. "I could have developed an inferiority complex. It seemed like everybody was betting on the horse."

But he won the first race by a nose. "When the man said go, I went," Flowers explained. "The horse or the rider had to think about it." The horse won the second night, setting up the grand finale. Flowers showed up riding the horse in a make-shift parade. Then, "I got the jump on him again, but I could hear him coming," Flowers said. "I remember wondering what would happen if that horse decided to run in my lane." He didn't, and Flowers won the strangest race of his life.

Hit the ground running—every morning that's what you do. You run errands; you run through a presentation; you give someone a run for his money; you always want to be in the running and never run-of-the-mill.

You're always running toward something, such as your goals, or away from something, such as your past. But you can never outrun yourself—or God. God keeps pace with you, call-ing you in the short run to take care of the long run by falling to your knees and running for your life—to Jesus.

I never get tired of running. The ball ain't that heavy.

—Herschel Walker

▶ **You can run to eternity by going to your knees.**

Rain Check

Read Genesis 9:1–17.

"I establish my covenant with you, that never again shall all flesh be cut off by the waters of a flood, and never again shall there be a flood to destroy the earth" (v. 11).

I s it really possible that rain could affect the outcome—of a basketball game?

Once upon a time, the University of Georgia had what was probably the worst facility in collegiate basketball—old Woodruff Hall. A. W. Davis was on the Volunteer team that made a trip to Athens in 1962 to play in the old barn. He told Marvin West in *Tales of the Tennessee Vols,* "In the beginning, we didn't take it too seriously when their coach, Red Lawson, told our coach, Ray Mears, that Georgia had the only gym in the country where weather might affect the game."

But the Vols discovered that the Georgia coach wasn't kidding after all. Some windows in the gym had been knocked out and had not been repaired. Sure enough, come game time it was raining.

Davis recalled, "We knew there was trouble when our manager issued football parkas for us to wear on the bench." Players had to dodge towels placed on the floor to blot the water that came in through the leaky roof. Davis devised a specific strategy for the game, consistently attempting to back the player guarding him "into one of the water hazards." Despite it all, the Vols won 87–84.

The kids are on go for their picnic. Your golf game is set. Friends are coming over to grill out. And then it rains.

Sometimes you make do in spite of a downpour, as Georgia and Tennessee did. But often the rain simply washes away your carefully laid plans. Rain falls when it wants to, without asking you if it's a convenient time. It answers only to God, the one who controls the heavens from which it comes, the ground on which it falls, and everything in between—territory that should include you. Is God in control of your life?

> *Don't pray when it rains if you don't pray*
> *when the sun shines.*
> —PITCHER AND PHILOSOPHER LEROY "SATCHEL" PAIGE

⋙ **While God controls the rain, he controls your life only if you choose to let him. Will you?**

The Testing Time

Read 1 Peter 4:12–16.

"Beloved, do not be surprised at the fiery ordeal that is taking place among you to test you, as though something strange were happening to you" (v. 12).

"**G**et it right, get it right. None of us wants him over here."

The "us" was the Tennessee football players and assistant coaches. The "him," according to Ward Gossett's *Volunteers Handbook,* was head coach Johnny Majors.

They didn't want Majors coming "over here" because this was the testing time for Majors, his coaches, and his players, the darkest hours of their football days in Knoxville. It was the second half of the 1988 season, and the days were growing shorter as the football season grew longer. Preseason favorites to win the SEC, the Vols were an unbelievable 0-6.

But, Gossett said, Majors was determined no one was going to quit. So he "went on a tear on the practice field, . . . and players and coaches alike quivered when they'd hear him trigger his bullhorn from high atop his platform. They knew when he keyed the bullhorn's trigger what was coming."

What was coming was "Check! Check! Check!" Majors would "shriek" the word, demanding that something be run again. If it wasn't to his liking, he "would come tearing down the platform steps to set it right."

Life often seems to be one battery of tests after another: high-school and college final exams, college entrance exams, the driver's license test, professional certification exams. They all stress us out because they measure our competency, and we fear that we will be found wanting.

But life itself is one long test, which means some parts are bound to be hard. Viewing life as an ongoing exam may help you keep your sanity, your perspective, and your faith when troubles come your way. After all, God is the proctor, but he isn't neutral; he's pulling for you to pass.

That 0-6 team ripped off five straight wins. They rededicated themselves and salvaged some gridiron glory. They were tested, and they passed.

Success is never permanent, and failure is never final.
—MIKE DITKA

> **Life is a test that God wants you to ace.**

Smiling Faces

Read Philippians 4:4–7.

"Rejoice in the Lord always; again I will say, Rejoice" (v. 4).

Willie Gault was not just one of the greatest athletes ever to wear the orange and white. He had more going for him than skill.

Wikipedia calls Gault "the prototypical 'speed merchant,' meaning his greatest asset was his pure straight-line swiftness." He was a football all-American in 1982, an NCAA champion in the sixty-yard indoor dash and the hurdles, and a member of an NCAA-champion relay team. In Super Bowl XX Gault led the victorious Chicago Bears with four receptions for 129 yards.

Yes, Willie Gault is one of the greatest Vols ever—but he's also one of the nicest.

In *Tales of the Tennessee Vols,* Marvin West wrote that Gault "had the whole package, the looks of a matinee idol, world-class speed, a keen mind, and a smile that could put Magic Johnson to shame."

That smile says a lot about Gault. It has served him well in Hollywood, where he has appeared on TV shows such as *The*

West Wing and in such movies as *The Sum of All Fears*. With the Bears he was, as West put it, "a misfit, a gentleman of distinction and class" on the same field with a quarterback who "drank beer and mooned helicopters."

What does your smile say about you? What makes you smile? Your dad's corny jokes? Don Knotts as Barney Fife? Your children or grandchildren? Your pal's bad imitations? And do you hoard your smile, or do you—like Willie Gault— give it away easily?

When you smile, the ones who love you and whom you love can't help but return the favor—and the joy. It's like turning on a bright light in a world threatened by darkness. Besides, you have good reason to walk around all the time with a smile on your face because of one basic, unswerving truth: God loves you.

> *Just play. Have fun. Enjoy the game.*
> —Michael Jordan

⫸ **It's so overused it's become a cliché, but it's true nevertheless: Smile! God loves you.**

A House Fit for a King

Read 2 Samuel 7:1–7.

*"Go and tell my servant David: Thus says the LORD: . . . I
have not lived in a house since the day I brought up the
people of Israel from Egypt to this day, but I have been
moving about in a tent and a tabernacle" (vv. 5–6).*

Those who see a Tennessee home baseball game are visiting
a true field of dreams when they enter Lindsey Nelson Stadium.

A new era began on February 23, 1993, when the stadium
opened for the first time. The article "Lindsey Nelson Stadium"
described this little jewel. The fans are close to the action, the
seating elevated so any seat in the house affords a complete
view of the field. No UT fan can complain about missing any
of the action.

Lindsey Nelson Stadium isn't just an idyllic site from which
to watch the perennial powerhouse Vols play ball; it's also a
state-of-the-art facility. For instance, the scoreboard includes a
video screen. Both the players and the press get the VIP treat-
ment with the diamond Vols having the run of a spacious equip-
ment room that, among its amenities, includes a video room, a

hitting tunnel, a pitcher's mound, and a lounge area complete with flat-screen TV, a pool table, and a Ping-Pong table.

Whether it's the beauty of the field or the quality of the play (or both), UT baseball fans turn out by the thousands to put Tennessee among the annual NCAA attendance leaders. Those fans and players who have never known anything but this beautiful park may take it for granted, but the stadium is the result of dedication, sacrifice, devotion, and a conviction that the Volunteers deserve only the best.

While you may feel that you, too, deserve only the best when it comes to your personal playing field, you may not see a field of dreams when you look into a mirror. Too heavy, too short, too pale, too brunette—we compare ourselves to an impossible standard Hollywood and fashion magazines have created, and we are inevitably disappointed.

Someone must have liked your body, though, because someone created it. That someone is God, who personally fashioned your unique, one-of-a-kind body and then gave it to you. Your body is a house fit for a king—the King.

> *If you don't do what's best for your body, you're the one who comes up on the short end.*
> —JULIUS ERVING

> **You may not have a fine opinion of your body, but God thought enough of it to personally create it for you.**

No Turning Back

Read Matthew 8:18–22.

"Jesus said to him, 'Follow me, and let the dead bury their own dead'" (v. 22).

Gradually Tamika Catchings came to realize there was no turning back.

In *Raise the Roof,* Pat Summitt wrote of Catchings's long ride from Texas to Knoxville as she set out to begin her college career in the fall of 1997. She was, of course, to be a part of the undefeated and national champion Lady Vols of 1997–98.

All of that was ahead of her, though, when she left home with her mom. Summitt said, "First, she was scared. Then, before she was even out of the state, she got homesick. Her mother was sitting right there next to her, but she already missed her."

When they crossed the Texas line, Catchings's mother saw her daughter tear up. Tamika finally said, "I hope I'm making the right decision."

What concerned Catchings was the great distance between Texas and Tennessee. As her mother and she covered the driving distance of fourteen and a half hours, she understood she would not be able to just stop by and see her mother. She could talk to her only on the phone, not in person.

Everything in her life would be different now. She was no longer a Texas high-school girl. She was a Tennessee Lady Volunteer. She had reached a point from which there was no turning back.

When you realize you've committed to something and there's no turning back, a combination of excitement and fear twists your gut into knots. Maybe it was the first time you went to camp and watched your parents drive away. The day you became a soldier. Your wedding day.

Commitment seems almost a dirty word in our society these days, a synonym for *chains,* an antonym for *freedom.* Perhaps we think Jesus is so scary because he demands commitment. But *commitment* actually means "purpose and meaning," especially when you're talking about your life. Commitment makes life worthwhile.

> *To finish first, you must first finish.*
> —Former racecar driver Rick Mears

> *Rather than constraining you, commitment lends meaning to your life, releasing you to move forward with purpose.*

The Leader

Read John 1:35–42.

"[Andrew] brought Simon to Jesus, who looked at him and said, 'You are Simon son of John. You are to be called Cephas' (which is translated Peter)" (v. 42).

A player is elected captain of a football team because he is a leader. In 1932 Malcolm Aitken demonstrated why the honor should be bestowed only upon a player who can step up when circumstances warrant.

The Vols were 8-0-1 when they headed to Jacksonville to play Florida. They needed a win for an outside chance at the Southern Conference championship. If ever a team was distracted, though, it was Tennessee. Russ Bebb wrote in *The Big Orange,* the players "were virtually certain that [coach Bob] Neyland was coaching his final game." Then, the night before the game, Neyland learned that his mother had died, and he left the team immediately for Greenville, Texas.

Bebb quoted *Knoxville Journal* sports editor Bob Murphy: "No Tennessee team ever displayed a poorer spirit than the Vols" until they got word that the coach's mother had died. Then Malcolm Aitken "showed the stuff that real men are made of." Under Aitken's leadership, the team held a secret meeting and vowed to "go out and pay a debt of respect and gratitude to one of the greatest coaches football has ever known."

The Vols demolished Florida 32–13. When South Carolina stunned Auburn with 20–20 tie, UT became conference champion.

The early Christian church found just such a leader in Simon Peter.

In *Twelve Ordinary Men,* John MacArthur described Simon as "ambivalent, vacillating, impulsive, unsubmissive." Yet he became, according to MacArthur, "the greatest preacher among the apostles" and the "dominant figure" in the birth of the church.

The implication for your own life is obvious and unsettling. You may think you lack the attributes necessary to make a good leader for Christ. But consider Simon Peter, an ordinary man who allowed Christ to rule his life and became the foundation upon which the Christian church was built.

Discover the talent that God has given you. Then go out and make the most out of it.
—Steve Spurrier

▶ **Men and women who allow Jesus to rule their lives are anything but ordinary.**

Cuss Words

Read Psalm 19:14.

"Let the words of my mouth and the meditation of my heart be acceptable to you, O LORD" (v. 14).

In 1921 Tennessee got "rooked" by Dartmouth.

The Volunteers went up to New Hampshire to play, their first venture into the East, which had for years been the home of college football powerhouses. UT lost that game 14–3, but some of the players didn't feel they got a fair shake.

Roy "Pap" Striegel—who never had the faintest idea how he got that nickname or what it meant—told Russ Bebb in *The Big Orange,* "We all figured we got rooked in that game." Striegel knew this was so because of the answer he was given when he asked the referee why he called back a Volunteer touchdown. He was told the right guard was offside. Striegel answered that couldn't possibly be true: "I'm playing right guard, and I pulled to run interference."

The Vols did manage to get away with some trespasses in the game. Striegel said Charlie Lindsay "played tackle, and he had a pretty good vocabulary of four-letter words. Anyway, all during that game, every time the referee turned around, Charlie would look him right in the eye and say 'you Yankee ————.' He did it right in the referee's face and got away with it."

We live in a coarsened culture where words no one would utter in polite society a few decades ago now spew from our music and our television sets—and our own mouths. Honestly answer these indelicate questions: With what name did you christen that slow driver you couldn't pass? What unflattering words did you have for that stubborn golf ball that wouldn't stay in the fairway?

Some argue that profane language is really harmless expression. Our words, however, reveal what's in our hearts, and what God seeks there is love and gentleness, not vileness.

> *American professional athletes are bilingual; they speak*
> *English and profanity.*
> —NHL LEGEND GORDIE HOWE

> **Our words—including profane ones—expose what's in**
> **our hearts.**

Choices

Read Deuteronomy 30:15–20.

"I have set before you life and death, blessings and curses. Choose life so that you and your descendents may live" (v. 19).

Why did Peyton Manning choose to play football at Tennessee rather than at Ole Miss, his legendary father's alma mater?

As Marvin West pointed out in *Tales of the Tennessee Vols,* the recruiting reception room at Ole Miss is named after Archie Manning, Peyton's dad and the most famous player in Rebel football history. Peyton's mom was a Mississippi homecoming queen. His brother Cooper was already on scholarship there.

Peyton said that had he gone to Oxford, no matter how well he played, "he would never have been as good 'as the people think I am.'" His father's shadow was just too big.

Still, Ole Miss beckoned, and Peyton panicked just before he made his final decision. He even asked his dad to tell him where he should play, but Archie demurred. Eventually, though, the younger Manning knew, and he had some powerful inside help with his decision. "You pray a lot, and you just know what you're going to do," he said.

By the way, little brother Eli knew ahead of anyone else—maybe even Peyton—that the decision would be for Tennessee. What was the source of Eli's insight? Logic. He looked at the rosters and figured Peyton would choose Tennessee because the Volunteers had better receivers.

Your life is the sum of the choices you've made. Your love of the Vols. Your spouse, or the absence of one. Your job, your home, even your pet. Your choices define you. That includes faith—or the lack of it. God lets you choose, though he reminds you that his way is life and that choosing against him is death.

Diehard Volunteer fans may argue, even in Peyton Manning's case, that the choice between Tennessee and Ole Miss was really no dilemma. And if your options are life or death, can there really be any question which you should choose?

You're the only person who can decide where you want to go and how you're going to get there.
—TERRY BOWDEN

▷ **God gives you the freedom to choose: life or death. What will you do?**

Wise, Innocent, and Ready

Read Matthew 10:5–23.

"See, I am sending you out like sheep into the midst of wolves; so be wise as serpents and innocent as doves" (v. 16).

While he was at Tennessee, Luke Hochevar had the natural, God-given talent every great baseball pitcher needs. But he also had an extraordinary something extra that separated him from other pitchers.

Hochevar worked his magic for the Vols through the 2005 season with a four-seam fastball that hit 96 mph, a sinking fastball, a hard-breaking slider, and a great curve. In 2005 he was the SEC Pitcher of the Year; he was 15-3 with an ERA of 2.26. He won the Roger Clemens Award as college baseball's top pitcher. Coach Rod Delmonico told Dana Heiss Grodin of *USA Today* that Hochevar was "as good as I've ever had here."

But when Hochevar pitched, he brought more than just ability: He went to the mound prepared. Grodin said every time Hochevar pitched, he asked himself, "Have I done everything I possibly can to prepare for this start? Not just prepared, but more prepared than every other pitcher? And I've never said no."

According to Grodin, Hochevar prepared mentally by twice visualizing the game he was to pitch and once by throwing a bullpen game. He also prepared himself physically with passionate work in the weight room. Some might argue he overanalyzed and overprepared, but the results at Tennessee speak for themselves.

You know the importance of preparation in your own life. You went to the bank for a car loan with the facts and figures in hand. The presentation you made at work was seamless because you practiced. The kids' school play suffered no meltdowns because they rehearsed. Knowing what you need to do and doing what you must to succeed isn't luck; it's preparation.

Jesus understood this, and he prepared his followers by lecturing them and by sending them on field trips. Two thousand years later, the life of faith requires similar training and study. After all, one day you'll see God face-to-face. You certainly want to be prepared.

Spectacular achievements are always preceded by unspectacular preparation.
—ROGER STAUBACH

> **Living in faith requires constant study and training, preparation for the day when you'll meet God face-to-face.**

A Dog's Life

Read Genesis 6:11–22; 8:1–4.

*"God remembered Noah and all the wild animals and
all the domestic animals that were with him in the ark"
(v. 8:1).*

He's described as one of the most beloved figures in the
state. He's certainly one of the most recognizable. He's
Smokey, the bluetick coonhound who is the Volunteers
mascot.

For today's Tennessee fans Smokey is so synonymous with
UT football that they can't imagine one without the other, but
the hound hasn't always been on the sidelines or leading the
Vols out of the giant T at each home game.

The article "Mascot: Smokey" relates how Smokey was
chosen. In 1953 the students declared in a poll that they wanted
a live mascot, so a contest was held to select a coonhound, a
breed of dog native to Tennessee, as that mascot. The late Rev-
erend Bill Brooks entered his prize-winning bluetick coonhound, whose distinguished real name was Brooks' Blue
Smokey.

The contest was held at halftime of the Mississippi State

game that year. As each dog was introduced, the students cheered for their favorites. Smokey was the last entry, and when his name was called, he barked. Not surprisingly, this fired the students up, and they cheered loudly. Smokey responded by throwing his head back and barking again. He kept going until he had the whole stadium in an uproar—and a Tennessee legend was born.

Do you have a dog or two around the place? How about a cat? Kids have gerbils?

We share our living space with animals we pamper and protect as well as with some—like roaches—we seek to exterminate. None of us, though, has the animal problems Noah did when he packed God's menagerie into one boat. God saved all creatures from extinction, including the fish, who were probably quite delighted with the whole flood business. All living things are under God's care.

It's not just icons like Smokey that we're responsible to care for and respect; it's all of God's creatures.

I like dogs better [than people]. With people, you never know which ones will bite.
—Diver Greg Louganis

▷ **God cares about all his creatures, and he expects us to respect them too.**

One Thing for Sure

Read Romans 8:28–30.

"We know that all things work together for good for those who love God, who are called according to his purpose" (v. 28).

Tennessee once played a game against Georgia Tech that remains, to this day, a matter of dispute as to who won.

This strangest of games was played on October 19, 1907, in Atlanta. Russ Bebb recounted the "great dispute" in *The Big Orange*. Tennessee attempted to punt from its five-yard line. The snap from center was low, and what happened next is the center of the dispute. It's unclear whether the kick was shanked or blocked. Either way, Tech recovered the ball after it scooted out of bounds behind the Volunteer goal line.

The referee first signaled safety for a 2–0 Tech lead. Tech protested, and the decision was changed, awarding Tech a touchdown and a 6–0 lead because the rules decreed a touchdown in the case of a blocked kick. Tennessee contended the kick was not blocked at all and that the call should be a safety.

The final score wound up 6–4 Tech. Or did it? Tennessee protested to the national rules committee. One paper reported a 4–2 Vol win, and sportswriter Grantland Rice called for a declaration of "no contest." The rules committee eventually passed the buck back to the referee, who declared Tech the winner. The conference, however, awarded the win to the Vols. The dispute has never been resolved.

Football games aren't played on paper. That is, you attend a Tennessee game expecting the Vols to win, but you don't know for sure. If you did, why bother to go?

Life doesn't get played on paper either. You never know what's going to happen tomorrow or even an hour from now. You may have a pretty good idea that you'll be at work Monday morning, but you never know for sure where you'll be or what you'll be doing. You can know, however, about forever. Life is uncertain, but eternity is a sure thing because it's in God's hands.

Recruiting is and always will be an inexact and highly speculative science.
—FRANK BROYLES

> **Life is unpredictable, and tomorrow is uncertain. Only eternity is a sure thing—because God controls it.**

Looking to the Lord

Read Micah 7:5–7.

"As for me, I will look to the Lord, I will wait for the God of my salvation" (v. 7).

"**W**e need a winner."

Such was the cry of the Orange Nation after the 1963 season, the sixth straight in which the Vols had failed to win more than six games. The athletic board agreed, but they couldn't decide on a coach to rally behind.

The board finally decided to let Bob Woodruff, the athletics director, do the picking. In *The Big Orange,* Russ Bebb called their move "one of the wisest decisions in athletic board annals." Woodruff recommended to the board thirty-one-year-old Doug Dickey, an assistant at Arkansas who had played quarterback for Woodruff when he was the head coach at Florida.

Dickey still had to win over the board, and one meeting did the job. According to one board member, "From the moment I first laid eyes on Dickey, I knew we had scored a bull's-eye." Why was the board member convinced Tennessee had a winner? "He had a way about him that inspired confidence.

You could sit there in that board meeting, listen to what he had to say, and realize instantly that he had the authority of command in him."

Dickey inspired confidence in others through his own self-confidence. The rest is UT football history: a 46-15-4 record and two SEC championships.

You need confidence in all areas of your life. You're confident the company you work for will pay you on time, or you wouldn't go to work. You turn the ignition, confident your car will start. When you flip a switch, you expect the light to come on. Confidence in other people and in things is often misplaced, though. Companies go broke; car batteries die; light bulbs burn out.

So where can you place your trust with absolute confidence you won't be betrayed? In God. He will not fail you; he will never let you down.

> *When it gets right down to the woodchopping, the key to winning is confidence.*
> —Darrell Royal

> **People, things, and organizations will let you down. Only God can be trusted absolutely and confidently.**

Fathers and Sons

Read Matthew 3:13–17.

"A voice from heaven said, 'This is my Son, the Beloved, with whom I am well pleased'" (v. 17).

The most storied father-and-son combination in Tennessee sports history almost wound up at different schools.

Allan Houston left UT as the school's all-time leading scorer, setting the record on December 9, 1992, against Syracuse. Randy Moore noted in *Hoop Tales: Tennessee Volunteers Men's Basketball* that after the record-breaking basket, the game ball was presented to Allan, who bounced it toward the Vol bench, where it was fielded by his father, Wade, the UT head coach.

Wade Houston was an assistant coach at Louisville Allan's senior year in high school, and for this reason Allan was not recruited, even though he was a consensus high-school all-American. Everyone assumed he was going to Louisville to be with his father; they were right. He signed with Louisville his senior year.

But during the spring of 1989, something happened: Wade got the head coaching job at Tennessee. Allan "knew immediately" he was going to Tennessee to be with his dad. He just had to find a way. "We all prayed about it," Allan said, and fortunately for the unity of the Houston family and for the fans of the Big Orange, the NCAA took note of the special circumstances and released Allan from his letter of intent. Father and son would be together in Knoxville.

You love your dad and make sure you eat dinner with him every Father's Day. Or maybe you don't talk to him if you can avoid it. You may not even know where he is and don't really care. But have you used your relationship with your father— loving, tempestuous, or nonexistent—to learn how to interact with your own son or daughter?

A model for the perfect relationship between a father and his children does exist: that of Jesus the Son and God the Father. You can look to their relationship for guidance and direction.

My dad was a huge influence on me. I imagine if he had put a wrench in my hand I would have been a great mechanic.
—PETE MARAVICH

➤ **Fatherhood is a tough job, but a model for the father-child relationship is found in that of Jesus the Son with God the Father.**

Going Fishing

Read Mark 1:16–20.

"Jesus said to them, 'Follow me and I will make you fish for people'" (v. 17).

Tennessee's football lore has at least a couple of fishing stories that, unlike most such tales, aren't whoppers at all—just the plain truth.

Randy Sanders, who was Tennessee's offensive coordinator from the national championship game against FSU in 1999 until the middle of the 2005 season, is a passionate fisherman. But he always fishes alone. It's by choice. Sanders told Marvin West in *Tales of the Tennessee Volunteers,* "When I'm fishing, I don't have all those people critiquing how I set the hook. If I miss a fish, I don't have to hear about it all week on the radio." His job was public; his hobby is private.

Another fishing story West recounted illustrates how tight General Bob Neyland was with money when he was athletics director. Mickey O'Brien served as the trainer from 1938 to 1972. He was a devoted angler who went to Florida each February to fish. Neyland knew about the trips, and O'Brien recalled that the AD would call him into his office before he set out.

Neyland would say something like, "While you're down there, run over to Jacksonville and see this boy. He may be a player. I'll pay your mileage—one way." But only one way.

If you fish, think back to the worst fishing trip you ever had. Maybe it was cold. You had a flat tire on the way. You got soaked and nearly froze. You didn't catch a thing. You got home late and got fussed at. It was still better than a good day at work, wasn't it?

What if somebody in authority looked you square in the eyes and told you, "Go fish"? How quickly would you trip over anybody who got in your way? Well, somebody did give you that assignment. Jesus said to go and fish for people who are drowning without him.

Some go to church and think about fishing; others go fishing and think about God.
—Fisherman Tony Blake

> **Jesus understood the passion people have for fishing and commanded that it become not just a hobby but a way of life.**

The Grudge

Read Matthew 6:7–15.

"If you forgive others their trespasses, your heavenly Father will also forgive you; but if you do not forgive others, neither will your Father forgive your trespasses" (vv. 14–15).

In *Hoop Tales: Tennessee Volunteers Men's Basketball,* Randy Moore wrote of a time when "practice lasted a little longer. The drills grew a little tougher. The coach's mood became a little gruffer." The reason for all the intensity? The next opponent was the Kentucky Wildcats, and the UT coach at the time was John Mauer.

For Mauer the game against Kentucky wasn't just a matter of beating the perennial SEC power and legendary coach Adolph Rupp. For Mauer the game was personal.

Mauer took over the reins at Tennessee before the 1938–39 season. Formerly he had been the head coach at Kentucky, where he rolled up a 40-14 record. He was fired to make way for a young coach whom the Kentucky brass figured had what it took to escalate the Wildcat program. That coach was Rupp.

Moore wrote, "Mauer exited quietly but grudgingly, and he carried the grudge to his grave." Bill Wright, one of Mauer's players, recalled, "You could tell from the way Mauer talked that he didn't care too much for Rupp." That grudge and the chance to whip Rupp may well have been why he bolted his successful program at Miami of Ohio to coach on The Hill. He did whip Rupp pretty consistently, going 7-8 against him through 1945.

You can probably recall times when somebody did you wrong. Does the memory still drive up your blood pressure? Or do you shrug it off as a lesson learned? Jesus said to forgive others, which is certainly easier said than done. But you are to forgive for your sake, not for the sake of the one who injured you. Without forgiveness the hurt festers, spreading its infection. When you forgive, the damage is over and done with. You can move on without pain.

Holding a grudge is a way to self-destruction. Forgiving and forgetting is a way of life.

Life is short, so don't waste any of it carrying around a load of bitterness. It only sours your life, and the world won't pay any attention anyway.
—PAT DYE

Forgiving others frees you from your past, turning you loose to get on with your life.

Quiet Time

Read Zechariah 2.

"Be silent, all people, before the Lord; *for he has roused himself from his holy dwelling" (v. 13).*

Might may not make right, but it sure can induce some silence.

In *Tales of the Tennessee Vols,* Marvin West told of a football coaches' meeting interrupted by "loud music boiling in from the adjoining athletic dormitory." Head coach Johnny Majors reminded his coaches that the players were supposed to be studying and sent assistant coach Jim Dyar to secure some peace and quiet.

Dyar tracked the music to the basketball wing and Bernard King's room. Dyar told King about the situation and said, "Bernard was very understanding and immediately turned down the volume." No sooner, though, had Dyar sat down in the conference room than the music struck up again. So the coach set out again, wondering what would happen to him if King and he got into a brawl. As he put it, "Expendable assistant coach or the basketball all-American?" With whom would the university side?

So Dyar went to the football section and found middle guard Jim Noonan. According to Dyar, "Noonan hit King's door hard enough to shake the building." Noonan "walked across the room, unplugged the radio, . . . and tucked it under his arm like a football. In response to Bernard's mild protest, Noonan said, 'Later.'"

Quiet time had officially begun.

The television blares; the telephone shrieks; the dishwasher rattles. Outside, the roar of traffic assaults your ears; a siren screams until you wince; the garbage collectors bang and slam the cans around.

We live in a noisy world. Yet God does not join in the cacophony. He patiently waits for you to turn to him in serenity and in calm. In quiet time with God, you can discover his presence anew. You'll discover something remarkable: that God's being with you is not remarkable at all. He's always there; you just can't hear him most of the time over the world's noise.

It's a lot better to be seen than heard. The sun is the most powerful thing I know of, and it doesn't make much noise.
—BEAR BRYANT

▶ **God speaks in a whisper, not a shout, so you must listen carefully or you will miss his voice altogether.**

Getting Smart

Read 1 Kings 4:29–34; 10:23–11:4.

"King Solomon excelled all the kings of the earth in riches and in wisdom. The whole earth sought the presence of Solomon to hear his wisdom, which God had put into his mind" (vv. 10:23–24).

UT coach Ray Mears was so shrewd and crafty that a strategy he used against Florida during the 1969–70 season resulted in a rules change.

As Randy Moore told it in *Hoop Tales: Tennessee Volunteers Men's Basketball,* the Vols trailed the Gators with only seconds left in the game. The usual strategy was to foul and hope for a miss of one or both of the free throws. Mears, however, came up with a strategy that was unique, if not downright brilliant.

He called a time-out—which is no big deal. Except that Mears knew he had no time-outs left. So he was hit with a technical—which was exactly what he wanted.

"The rule at that time gave the opponent one free throw, then there was a jump ball," Mears told Moore. This meant, first of all, that the Gators would get only one free throw instead of two. But the Vols had six-ten Bobby Croft, so Mears figured the Vols would control the tip. It worked. Croft controlled every jump ball, and the Vols swapped one point for two by calling one time-out after another and getting hit with a series of technicals. They sent the game into overtime before losing.

The NCAA hastily closed the loophole Mears had exploited.

Remember that time you wrecked the car? That cold day you fell out of the boat? The morning you locked yourself out of the house or out of the truck? Smart, huh?

Our world often insists that great intelligence and scholarship are not compatible with faith in God. But any incompatibility happens only when we trust in our own wisdom rather than the wisdom of God. We forget, as Solomon did, that God is the ultimate source of all our knowledge and wisdom and that even our ability to learn is a gift from God.

I don't hire anybody not brighter than I am. If they're not smarter than me, I don't need them.
—BEAR BRYANT

▶ **Being truly smart means trusting in God rather than only in your own smarts.**

Payback

Read Matthew 5:38–42.

"I say to you, Do not resist an evildoer. But if anyone strikes you on the right cheek, turn the other also" (v. 39).

It was payback time on the football field—and the Vols made a mistake.

General Bob Neyland always scheduled a breather or two. In 1940 one such cupcake was Southwestern (today's Rhodes College), and the Vols romped 40–0 with Neyland substituting eleven players at a time throughout the game.

One starter, Val Thompson, was in long enough to get the daylights knocked out of him—or more literally, some teeth. He recalled to Haywood Harris and Gus Manning in *Six Seasons Remembered,* "I got hit twice on one play, losing some teeth on one hit and injuring my eye on the other."

As the Vols huddled up, another player asked Thompson who had hit him. He replied he thought it was the end. A few plays later the teammate knocked the end out of the game.

Standing up for and taking the side of a teammate in a football game is generally admired, even if it means revenge or payback, as was the case in the 1940 game against South-western.

Somebody's done you wrong—that driver who cut you off, a coworker who lied about you to the supervisor, your ex who cheated on you. Time to get even?

Resentment and anger hurt you and no one else. You're stewing in your own juices, poisoning your own happiness while that other person blithely goes on. The only way someone who has hurt you can keep hurting you is if you're a willing participant.

Jesus ushered in a new way of living when he taught that we are not to seek revenge for wrongs and injuries. What a relief!

And about that Southwestern game? Thompson said, "When we got home and looked at the film, we found it was the linebacker [not the end] who had done it." The Vols had exacted their revenge on the wrong player.

> *I think football would become an even better game if someone could invent a ball that kicks back.*
> —COMEDIAN ERIC MORECAMBE

> **Resentment and anger over a wrong injures you, not the other person, so forget it—just as Jesus taught.**

The *I* in Pride

Read 1 John 2:15–17.

"All that is in the world—the desire of the flesh, the desire of the eyes, the pride in riches—comes not from the Father but from the world" (v. 16).

His teammates tried to help Ron Widby achieve a record before he even knew it was within reach.

The Volunteer basketball team of 1966–67 won Tennessee's first SEC title in twenty-four years and earned the school's first NCAA Tournament bid ever. One of the highlights of this remarkable season occurred in the last home game of the season. The Vols could clinch a tie for the SEC crown with a win over LSU. Tennessee took a nice lead in the second half, and then, as Randy Moore put it in *Hoop Tales: Tennessee Volunteers Men's Basketball,* "Something downright bizarre happened."

Widby passed to a teammate, who immediately threw it right back to him. He passed to another teammate, who did the same thing. Widby then shot and scored. On the next possession the same thing happened. Widby passed; the teammate passed the ball back; Widby shot and scored.

Widby eventually figured out what was going on: "They wanted me to get the Fieldhouse scoring record." The record was forty-seven points, and thanks to Ron Widby's unselfish teammates, he broke the record, finishing with fifty points before taking a seat. The other players put their personal goals aside to help Widby achieve one he, in his own selflessness, had no intention of attaining.

What are you most proud of? The size of your bank account or the trophies from your tennis league? The title under your name at the office? Your family?

Pride is a paradox. You certainly want a surgeon who takes pride in her work or a Volunteer coach who is proud of his team's ability. But pride in the things of this world is inevitably disappointing, for it leads to dependence upon things that will pass away. Pride in the world's baubles lures you to the world and the temporary, and away from God and the eternal.

Southerners are proud of their football heritage, their schools, and their teams. And they share a deep pride that goes with being from the South.
—Former Volunteer announcer George Mooney

▶ **Pride can be dangerous because it tempts you to lower your sight from God and the eternal to the world and the temporary.**

Mysterious Ways

Read Romans 11:25–36.

"O the depth of the riches and wisdom and knowledge of God! How unsearchable are his judgments and how inscrutable his ways!" (v. 33)

The good Lord sure works in mysterious ways.

It's an old saying among people of faith, an acknowledgment of the limits of our understanding of God.

Coach Phillip Fulmer said it in his book *A Perfect Season*. The Vols had just lost to Nebraska in the 1998 Orange Bowl, and Fulmer wanted to get right to work on the next season. Instead, almost as soon as he arrived back in Knoxville from Miami, he had to head to California for the East-West Shrine Bowl Game to coach the East team. "I was really dreading it," Fulmer said. "I just hated leaving, period, because it meant I would be so far away from my work at Tennessee."

But then came the mysterious ways of the good Lord. The week turned into a blessing for the coach that was pivotal in Tennessee's drive to the national championship in the fall. Fulmer said the time far from home allowed him the chance to review what they needed to do to win a national championship.

He called the week "a real blessing . . . which I believe set in motion the direction of our 1998 football team."

Mysterious ways indeed.

Do you love a good whodunit or a rousing round of Clue? Do you match wits with Perry Mason in TV reruns? A lot of folks like a good mystery. They like the challenge of uncovering what somebody else wants to hide.

Some mysteries, though, are simply beyond our knowing. For instance, much about God remains mysterious. Why does he tolerate the existence of evil? What does he really look like? Why is he so fond of bugs?

We know for sure, though, that God is love, so we proceed with life, assured that one day all mysteries will be revealed.

Through sports, a coach can offer a boy a way to sneak up on the mystery of manhood.

—Writer Pat Conroy

▷ **God chooses to keep much about himself shrouded in mystery, but one day we will see and understand.**

DAY 40

Amazing!

Read Luke 23:26–24:12.

"Why do you look for the living among the dead? He is not here, but has risen" (v. 24:5).

ondredge Holloway had many magical and amazing moments in his three years of varsity ball, quarterbacking the Vols to a 25-9-2 record from 1972 to 1974. His most amazing day of all, though, was one in which he missed most of the game because of an injury.

In the 1974 opener against UCLA, Holloway suffered a separated shoulder in the first quarter. He left the field in an ambulance, presumably gone for the season.

UCLA led 17–10 in the fourth quarter. And then, as Randy Moore related in *Stadium Stories: Tennessee Volunteers,* "Suddenly an eerie hush fell over the assembled multitude, as though all 70,000 observers were struck speechless. Then came a murmur . . . that quickly exploded into a thunderous roar."

Amazingly, Holloway had returned to the Tennessee sidelines. Even more amazingly, he then trotted onto the field. For the Vols, "Their conquering hero had returned in time to save the day."

Amazingly, he did just that. With an injured shoulder, he led the Vols on an eighty-yard march. He then scored from the two-yard line, "acrobatically somersault[ing] into the end zone, landing head first to tie the score at 17-all." It wasn't a win, but the Tennessee faithful who were there that day felt otherwise. And they knew they had witnessed something truly amazing.

The word *amazing* defines the limits of what you believe to be plausible or usual. The Grand Canyon, the birth of your children, that chocolate-whipped-cream-raspberry dessert, those last-second Volunteer wins—they're amazing!

The really amazing aspect of your life, though, is not the sights you've seen, the places you've been, the people you've met and loved, or the things you've experienced. All that—everything—pales beside God's walking around on Earth, letting people kill him, and then not staying dead.

Most amazing of all is the reason God did such things: because he loves you.

Football is an incredible game. Sometimes it's so incredible, it's unbelievable.

—TOM LANDRY

> **God let humans kill him—and then refused to stay dead. That's amazing, but the best part is that he did it for you.**

At the Last Trumpet

Read 1 Corinthians 15:50–58.

"The trumpet will sound, and the dead will be raised im-perishable, and we will be changed" (v. 52).

In his book *Tales of the Tennessee Vols,* Marvin West wrote of one of the more interesting assignments handed assistant coach Gerald Oliver while Ray Mears was head coach of the men's basketball team. Oliver was center Rupert Breedlove's personal wake-up call.

Breedlove failed his preseason speed and endurance tests and thus was ordered to make early morning runs. As low man on the coaching totem pole, Oliver was given the delightful job of meeting Breedlove on the track every morning at five-thirty.

Breedlove failed to show on the second morning, though, so Oliver dutifully launched a thorough search. West said, "The dining hall wasn't open. Nobody was in the showers. The coach went to the player's room. No Rupert in sight."

Befuddled but determined, Oliver looked under the bed. No way the big center could fit under there. Finally, as he was about to go away, Oliver checked the closet. There stood Breedlove. According to the story, the center's "first words as he wiggled out from behind his clothes were 'Sometimes I sleep in the closet.'"

There was just no avoiding the human wake-up call that was coach Gerald Oliver. When he showed up, it was getting-up time for Rupert Breedlove.

Like Breedlove, you may feel that being roused out of bed in the morning is not among the great joys of your life—even if you don't hide in the closet as a ploy to grab some extra sleep. You may well agree that the alarm clock is history's most sadistic invention.

But imagine being awakened to a trumpet shrieking in your ear—and being overjoyed about it! The last trumpet blast is the blaring and clarion call of the one final and true wake-up call when Jesus will round up the faithful. No one will ever need an alarm clock again.

He's a guy who gets up at six o'clock in the morning
regardless of what time it is.
—BOXING TRAINER LOU DUVA

>> **God will sound a final wake-up call at which even the sleepiest will arise.**

The Word

Read John 1:1–18.

"In the beginning was the Word, and the Word was with God, and the Word was God. . . . And the Word became flesh and lived among us" (vv. 1, 14).

Trash talking is not something invented by the vociferous and boastful athletes of modern times. In fact, one of the best trash talkers Tennessee has ever had was DeWitt Weaver, captain of the 1936 football team.

The team finished only 6-2-2, not great by UT standards. Thus, the Vols were decided underdogs when one of Duke's greatest teams ever came calling at Shields-Watkins. On this homecoming day in Knoxville, Duke, as one of college football's top two teams, had its eyes on the Rose Bowl.

Weaver saw things differently, and he was not shy about letting Duke know what he thought—particularly Duke's mammoth end, Dick Talliaferro. According to Russ Bebb in *The Big Orange,* Weaver repeatedly shouted across the line to Talliaferro, "We're not going to let you guys go to the Rose Bowl." At first Talliaferro returned the favor, shouting back at Weaver, "We're going to beat you fifty points." That only turned the heat up for other UT players, who razzed the Blue Devil the rest of the game. And as Bebb put it, every time Weaver talked trash, "Talliaferro seemed to get more incensed."

DeWitt Weaver had the first and the last word that day when UT pulled off a 15–13 upset behind a late seventy-yard punt return by Red Harp.

A blind date. A job interview. A twenty-year class reunion. New neighbors. You want to make an impression—preferably a good one. How do you influence people to form the opinion you want them to? By your words and your actions.

God gave us an impression of himself in exactly the same way. In Jesus, God took the unprecedented step of making his Word flesh and bone. We now know for all time the sorts of things God does and the sorts of things God says. God came to make a good impression on you.

I broke in with four hits and the writers promptly decided they had seen the new Ty Cobb. It took me only a few days to correct that impression.
—CASEY STENGEL

▶ **God sent his Word—as Jesus—to make an impression on us.**

In God's Own Time

Read 2 Kings 6:24–33; 7.

"While he was still speaking with them, the king came down to him and said, 'This trouble is from the Lord! Why should I hope in the Lord any longer?'" (v. 6:33).

On December 16, 1909, as Randy Moore put it in *Hoop Tales: Tennessee Volunteers Men's Basketball,* all of two hundred people—a capacity crowd—"jammed into the cozy YMCA gymnasium on The Hill, eagerly anticipating an eight o'clock tip-off between the Volunteers and Kentucky Central (now Centre College)." The occasion was Tennessee's first-ever men's basketball game, which the Vols won 33–31.

On March 9, 1979, thousands of people jammed into the Murphy Center in Murfreesboro, eagerly anticipating a tip-off between the Volunteers and Eastern Kentucky. The occasion was the NCAA Tournament.

What made this night special was that the Vols won. They fell behind by ten early, before rallying to win going away 97–81. Moore quoted reserve Chuck Threets as proclaiming, "We made history! We did it!"

On that night the Vols ended seventy years of NCAA Tournament futility. Coach Don DeVoe expressed what the whole Orange Nation felt: "It was inconceivable to me that Tennessee, with all of the success it had experienced to that point, had never won an NCAA Tournament game."

On this night, they won their first—but certainly not their last. It had truly been a long time coming for the ever-hopeful Volunteer fans, players, and coaches.

How much time do you spend waiting? To get a table at a restaurant? To get your driver's license renewed? To see your doctor? But what about waiting for something you're not sure will ever come? Like a winning lottery ticket. Your ship to come in. Your big break in business—or even a job that pays enough to feed your family.

You may well lose faith in such things, but the ultimate source of all your hope is God. You can wait on God, knowing that his promises will be fulfilled—in God's own time.

I was born and raised on a farm, and when you watch those crops grow, you learn to be patient.
—PAT DYE

▷ **God moves in his own time, so often we must wait, remaining faithful and hopeful.**

Southern Hospitality

Read 2 Kings 4:8–17.

"Let us make a small roof chamber with walls, and put there for him a bed, a table, a chair, and a lamp, so that he can stay there whenever he comes to us" (v. 10).

"**W**elcome, y'all." Nice, but a smile and a handshake aren't enough.

Consider this: More than 26,000 students; 8,300 faculty and staff members; 550 acres; 220 buildings.

That's the University of Tennessee, and it's a big, bewildering place for a young person visiting for the first time. Sometime during that visit the campus must transform from cold and frightening to warm and hospitable. Especially if the young person in question is one of the best and the brightest athletes whose future most definitely should lie with the Volunteers. That's when good old Southern hospitality comes into play, and at Tennessee that means Orange Pride.

Alan Horne explained about Orange Pride in the article "Vol Hostess Program." Until 2005 they were known as hostesses: young women who helped the athletic department host recruits. When the name was changed to Orange Pride, though, the group's responsibilities increased. While they do most of their work with men's basketball and football, Orange Pride, which now includes men as well as women, helps recruit the nation's best players in other sports. They spend time with the recruits and their families, answering any questions about life at UT.

All in all, Orange Pride is a student group assigned the job of being goodwill ambassadors for the university by turning on the charm and the hospitality.

Southerners are deservedly famous for their hospitality. Down South, warmth and genuineness seem genetic. You open your home to the neighborhood kids, to your friends, to the stranger whose car broke down in the rain, to the stray cat that showed up hungry and hollering. You even let family members overstay their welcome without grumbling.

Your hospitality is a sign of a loving and generous nature, a touch of the divine in you. God, too, is a gracious host, and one day he will open the doors of his place for you—and never ask you to leave.

Being raised in the South means growing up on a diet of southern hospitality and a dose of football every weekend.
—ASKMEN.COM

▶ **Hospitality is an outward sign of the inward loving and generous nature of the host.**

Our Inheritance

Read Ephesians 1:3–14.

"He destined us for adoption as his children through Jesus Christ. . . . In Christ we have also obtained an inheritance" *(vv. 5, 11).*

In *Hoop Tales: Tennessee Volunteers Men's Basketball,* Randy Moore said Don DeVoe "inherited a coach's nightmare" when he came to Tennessee from Wyoming in 1978 to coach the men's basketball team.

The Vols had been only 6-12 in the SEC and 11-16 overall in 1977–78, so DeVoe knew the program was in trouble. It may have been worse than he expected. Moore said the squad "played no defense." The team had surrendered 121 and 101 points in a pair of losses to LSU and had lost 107–94 at Auburn. Moreover, the team's "best athlete . . . was known for turnovers and poor shot selection. The program's best post defender . . . was so grossly out of shape that he was banned from practice until he lost thirty-five pounds. And the team's most experienced player . . . found DeVoe's deliberate offense so confining that he lost his cool and his first-team job."

As Moore put it, the team DeVoe inherited was "long on

self-esteem and short on self-discipline." But this "coach's nightmare" finished the season 21-12, beat Kentucky three times, won the league tournament title by defeating those same Wildcats 75–69 in the finals, and advanced to the second round of the NCAA Tournament.

As Don DeVoe learned, some inheritances may be suspect. For instance, you had no say in who your relatives are or into what time you were born; you inherited both with the first breath you took on your own. Would you really keep all your kinfolk if you could throw some back? Does some kinder, gentler time beckon to you?

Your birthright, though, also included the greatest inheritance you could possibly receive: the one God has prepared for you through Jesus Christ.

> *[Football in the South is] part of our heritage, and that heritage is passed along from generation to generation.*
> —FRANK BROYLES

> **The fact of your birth made you an heir: You inherit your relatives, the world situation, and the gifts God gives you through Jesus.**

Throwing in the Towel

Read Numbers 13:25–14:4.

"The men who had gone up with him said, 'We are not able to go up against this people, for they are stronger than we'" (v. 13:31).

T oyin Olupona was ready to quit. The UT sprinter was injured her freshman year, got herself ready for her sophomore year, and then was injured again.

It was a dark time for the native of Canada. "I think my freshman year, when I got hurt, I was depressed because I was alone," she told Jeff Cohran of the *Daily Beacon*. Then, when she was hurt her sophomore year, she said, "I kinda gave up. I didn't want to have anything to do with track."

But her coaches and her parents didn't give up on her, and ultimately she didn't give up either. During the summer after her sophomore season, Olupona talked it over with her parents and the UT coaches, and she made a decision: "I can't stop. This is what God has given me, and when God gives you a talent, you gotta use it."

And did Olupona ever use that God-given talent! Rededicated to running and in partnership with God, she made the most of her last two years on The Hill. She completed her career at UT in 2005 as an all-American and SEC champion and a key member of the 2005 NCAA indoor track and field champions, Tennessee's first. She was twice runner-up in the NCAA sixty-meter dash. All because she didn't quit.

Remember that time you quit a high-school sports team? Bailed out of a relationship? Walked away from that job? How could you forget? You regret those unfinished parts of your life because you can't go back and complete them. All you can do now is ponder the possibilities of "What if?"

The next time you're tempted to give up on something or someone, remember the people of Israel who quit when the Promised Land was theirs for the taking. They forgot one fact of life you never should: God never gives up on you.

The first time you quit, it's hard. The second time, it gets easier. The third time, you don't even have to think about it.
—BEAR BRYANT

▷ **Whatever else you give up on in your life, don't give up on God. He will never ever give up on you.**

Cheap Tricks

Read Acts 19:11–20.

*"The evil spirit said to them in reply, 'Jesus, I know, and
Paul I know; but who are you?'" (v. 15).*

Stepping on another player to spring over the line of scrimmage? Sewing a harness into a back's jersey and sailing him
forward? In the rough-and-tumble early days of college football, the rules were vague, with holes in them that allowed for
downright outlandish and outrageous trick plays. Some of the
early coaches in Knoxville weren't averse to dreaming up and
pulling off a gadget play or two.

According to Ward Gossett in *Volunteers Handbook,* the first
recorded use of a trick play by the Volunteers came in 1901
against Alabama. During the game, the Tennessee players
padded the back of one of their own. He "was then used by another player as a stepping stone–like springboard to clear the
line of scrimmage."

Gossett related that the Vols used an even more innovative
trick play in the 1904 Alabama game, which Tennessee won 5–
0. Running back Sam McAllester "was equipped with a harness that featured handles on either side. As he ran toward the

line of scrimmage, a halfback on either side would grab hold of a handle and throw him over the line."

Trick plays have been around in Knoxville practically as long as has the Volunteer football team.

In life, scam artists are everywhere—and they love trick plays. An email encourages you to send money to some foreign country to get rich. That guy at your front door makes an offer to resurface your driveway that you can't refuse. A TV ad promises that a pill will help you lose weight without diet or exercise.

You've been around; you know that if something is too good to be true, it probably is. Many people approach Jesus the same way. His good news sounds too good to be true. But the only catch is that there is no catch.

No tricks—just the truth.

Anybody with ability can play in the big leagues. . . . To trick people year in and year out, the way I did, I think that was a much greater feat.

—Bob Uecker

God's promises sound too good to be true, but the only catch is that there is no catch.

Looking Ahead

Read Matthew 24:15–31.

"Take note, I have told you beforehand" (v. 25).

Nancy Lay could look around at the state of Lady Volunteers basketball today and say, "I told you so."

Lay was the person most responsible for reviving the disbanded women's basketball program at Tennessee in 1960. She was the first modern-day coach, leading the "Volettes," as they were then known, until 1968.

That was a different age. Haphazard recordkeeping makes an accurate account of those early seasons impossible, according to Randy Moore in *Hoop Tales: Tennessee Lady Volunteers*.

Perhaps it was a more pristine age. Lay recalled that one year they gave out toenail clippers for winning a tournament. "They were like a hundred for a dollar," she said. The players didn't have uniforms but wore shorts and T-shirts.

After the 1968 season, though she still enjoyed the job, Lay stepped aside. She saw massive changes coming, and she chose to teach. "I didn't want to get into big-time athletics," she said. "I knew what was coming; it was going to become a full-time job, and I didn't want that."

Nancy Lay was, of course, right on about her prediction for the future of women's basketball at Tennessee. It certainly became big-time, the greatest women's college basketball program of all.

Don't you just hate it when somebody says, "I told you so"? That means the other person was right and you were wrong. You could have listened to that know-it-all in the first place, but then you would have lost the chance yourself to crow, "I told you so."

Jesus told everybody exactly what he was going to do: come back and take his faithful with him. Those who don't listen will be left with those four awful words, "I told you so," ringing in their ears—and their souls.

There's nothing in this world more instinctively abhorrent to me than finding myself in agreement with my fellow humans.
—LOU HOLTZ

▷ *Jesus matter-of-factly told us what he has planned: He will return to gather all the faithful to himself.*

The Gift

Read Hebrews 10:1–18.

"This is the covenant that I will make with them after these days, says the LORD: . . . I will remember their sins and their lawless deeds no more" (vv. 16, 17).

On May 18, 1973, Tennessee demonstrated one of the most unusual and greatest acts of sportsmanship in history. Almost fifty-seven years after the fact, the Vols gave back a conference championship.

As Russ Bebb told it in *The Big Orange,* athletic officials pointed out that a 0–0 tie with Kentucky had kept Tennessee from tying for the championship of the Southern Intercollegiate Athletic Association in 1916. But as Bebb noted, the "odd thing is that Tennessee did not actually claim the championship in the first place." He cited newspapers and the Tennessee yearbook as evidence, with both conceding the title to Georgia Tech. The yearbook, in fact, congratulated Tech for edging the Vols for the conference title.

However, Bebb said, "along the way, UT's official records began to list 1916 as an SIAA championship year. So did Georgia Tech's." In 1973, though, the Vols conceded the title to

Tech, which was undefeated and untied in SIAA play. Tech and Tennessee did not play each other that year, so the scoreless tie with Kentucky on Thanksgiving Day kept the Vols from sharing the title. The public declaration was sportsmanship at its highest level, an act of giving performed solely because it was right, with no ulterior motives.

Receiving a gift is nice, but giving has its pleasures too, doesn't it? The children's excitement on Christmas morning. Your spouse's smile of sheer delight for that really cool anniversary present. Your dad's surprise that time you didn't give him a tie or socks.

You may even enjoy visiting the mall occasionally and shopping for that just-right gift, allowing yourself a little pride in your generosity.

The greatest gift-giver of all, though, is God. He gave you everything you have, including your life. What, then, could you possibly give him in return? Your love and your life.

Why is there only one ball for twenty-two players? If you gave a ball to each of them, they'd stop fighting for it.
—SOURCE UNKNOWN

≫ **Nobody can match God when it comes to giving, but you can give him the gift of your love in return.**

The Big Time

Read Matthew 2:19–23.

"He made his home in a town called Nazareth" (v. 23).

Ray Bussard was as improbable a big-time swimming coach as there has ever been.

In *Tales of the Tennessee Vols,* Marvin West described Bussard's trip "from the backwoods to the big time" as done "over rocky roads, across muddy creeks and barbed-wire fences, through briars and tangles, always up hill."

Bussard truly did begin in the backwoods, wearing overalls in a one-room schoolhouse in Big Valley, Virginia. He truly did wind up in the big time, as coach of one of the most successful swimming programs in collegiate history. And in the big time, Bussard hit it big. Over his twenty-one years at Knoxville as head coach of the UT swimming team, he compiled a record of 252-20 that included a streak of eighty-five straight wins. His teams won eight SEC championships, finished in the top five in the NCAA championships eight straight times, and swam to the 1978 national title.

The country boy from the backwoods was a player on both the national and the international stage. He was twice the

NCAA Coach of the Year and was an Olympic coach in 1984. From Big Valley to Knoxville and the Olympics was a long way, but Bussard made the journey and flourished.

Like Ray Bussard, you may have been born by a bump in the road and grown up in a virtually unknown village in a backwater county. Perhaps you started out on a stage far removed from the bright lights of Broadway, the glitz of Hollywood, or the halls of power in Washington, D.C. Those original circumstances don't have to define or limit you, though, for life is much more than geography. It is about character and walking with God wherever you go.

A small-town boy himself, Jesus knew all about that.

Where you are doesn't matter. What you are does.

I live so far out in the country that I have to walk toward town to go hunting.
—Former major leaguer Rocky Bridges

▶ **Where you live may largely be the culmination of a series of circumstances; what you are is a choice you make.**

Resting Easy

Read Hebrews 4:1–11.

"A sabbath rest still remains for the people of God; for those who enter God's rest also cease from their labors as God did from his. Let us therefore make every effort to enter that rest" (vv. 9–11).

Kristen "Ace" Clement was a star freshman for the 1997–98 national champion Lady Vols. One of the most highly recruited players in the country, the point guard had broken Wilt Chamberlain's all-time Philadelphia high-school scoring mark.

Coach Pat Summitt described Clement in *Raise the Roof* as "a glamorous left-handed point guard . . . with a floppy ponytail and an almost illusory passing ability, a sleight-of-hand artist who could make the ball seem to flicker around the court." The Lady Vols needed that ability badly. Summitt flatly declared, "We couldn't lose Ace."

So what happened? She got hurt before her freshman season even started.

It began as a sore foot, but the pain worsened, especially after the relentless freshman defied the pain and kept running. Clement thought the pain would go away if she just didn't tell anyone. But it didn't. Finally she gave in and told trainer Jenny Moshak, "My foot hurts." An MRI delivered the bad news: Clement had a stress fracture.

That was bad enough for Clement, whom Summitt called "obsessively dedicated" to basketball. Perhaps even worse was the rehabilitation routine prescribed: time and complete rest. Ace Clement had to take a break.

Rest is important to maintain physical—and spiritual— health. Rest for you may mean a good eight hours in the sack. Or a Saturday morning that begins in the backyard with the paper and a pot of coffee. Or a vacation in the mountains, where the most strenuous thing you do is change position in the hot tub.

God promised you rest of a particular kind. His rest comes through faith: As you spend your day in the presence of God, you are revitalized and rejuvenated. The world around you may degenerate into chaos, but your soul remains at peace, at rest.

Eat hard, work harder, rest hardest.
—MAJOR LEAGUER JULIO FRANCO

▶ **God promises you rest that goes beyond eight hours in the sack or a day spent lounging in front of the TV.**

Going Out in Style

Read Deuteronomy 34.

"Moses went up . . . to the top of Pisgah, . . . and the LORD showed him the whole land: . . . Then Moses, the servant of the LORD, died there in the land of Moab, at the LORD's command. He was buried in a valley . . . but no one knows his burial place to this day" (vv. 1, 5–6).

Some marriages just don't last, but a messy divorce isn't inevitable.

Ken Donahue was the starting right offensive tackle on General Bob Neyland's 1949 team that went 7-2-1 and was ranked seventeenth. After coaching at UT for five years, he moved on to Mississippi State, where he shared an office with Johnny Majors. From there he went to Tuscaloosa and Bear Bryant's staff at Alabama, eventually moving up to assistant head coach and defensive coordinator.

But Bryant retired, and Majors called from Knoxville. He needed some help on the defensive side of the ball, and he wanted Donahue to provide that help. Marvin West wrote in *Tales of the Tennessee Vols,* "This was a celebrated marriage, Alabama's best assistant finally coming home."

The results were immediate. In 1985 Donahue's defense held Auburn's Bo Jackson to eighty yards in the second game of the season. The underdog Vols blasted Miami 35–7 in the Sugar Bowl. West said, "Donahue got the lion's share of the credit. His blitz package was too much for Vinny Testaverde."

But the marriage didn't last. Midway through the 1988 season, Majors and Donahue parted company after forty-two games. As fans clamored for Majors's head, Donahue resigned. West said the veteran coach "went away quietly. He was old-school. There would be no kicking and screaming."

You probably have known some times in your life when you felt it was necessary to move on. The job at which you had done all you could. The friendship that wasn't so close any more. That tearful handing of your daughter to your new son-in-law. Maybe even a marriage. Sometimes you have no choice about if or when something will end, but you can always choose whether you exit in style, like Ken Donahue—and the legendary leader Moses.

In the bigger picture, when it comes to life and death, going out in style means leaving with God's praise: "Well done, good and faithful servant."

> *Don't go to your grave with a life unused.*
> —BOBBY BOWDEN

⟩ **The only true way to go out in style is to leave this life with praise from God.**

A Gentleman and a Player

Read John 2:13–22.

"Making a whip of cords, he drove all of them out of the temple. . . . He also poured out the coins of the money changers and overturned their tables" (v. 15).

In his book *The Big Orange,* Russ Bebb pronounced Tennessee all-American back Beattie Feathers "one of the most popular players ever to play" for the Vols. Known as the antelope in orange, Feathers scored thirty-three touchdowns in the thirty games he played for UT. Bebb quoted the 1933 UT yearbook's salute of Feathers as "all-Southern, all-America and, above all, a gentleman on the gridiron. He played the game fair and square. He could take the dirty digs, but he didn't dish them out."

How could a gentleman survive in the rough-and-tumble and downright cutthroat game that was college football in the 1930s? Well, Feathers was a gentleman who played by the rules, but he was not soft.

The classic 1932 game against Alabama illustrates how tough Feathers was. It was played in a downpour that limited his running ability. Still, he kept Bama backed up all afternoon by averaging forty-six yards on twenty-three punts. Late in the game Alabama led 3–0, and the players were exhausted and just hanging on under the adverse conditions. But three plays after a short Bama punt, Feathers still had enough grit to push his way into the end zone for a 7–3 UT win.

A calm, caring manner and a soft voice are often taken for weakness, and gentle men are frequently misunderstood by those who fail to appreciate their inner strength. But Beattie Feathers's football career and Jesus's rampage through the Jerusalem temple illustrate the perils of underestimating a determined gentleman.

You understand that the best way to have a request honored is to make it civilly, with a smile. God works that way too. He could bully you and boss you around; you couldn't stop him. But instead he gently requests your attention, waiting for the courtesy of a reply.

> *Rugby is a beastly game played by gentlemen. Soccer is a gentleman's game played by beasts. Football is a beastly game played by beasts.*
> —HENRY BLAHA

God is a gentleman, soliciting your attention politely and then patiently waiting for you to give him the courtesy of a reply.

Never a Good Idea

Read Mark 14:43–50.

"The betrayer had given them a sign, saying, 'The one I will kiss is the man; arrest him and lead him away under guard'" (v. 44).

Shortly after Bridgette Gordon committed to playing basketball for Tennessee, she accepted a scholarship offer from Florida. That meant she crossed coach Pat Summitt.

Not a good idea.

By the time she left Knoxville in 1989, Gordon had led the Volunteers to four Final Fours and their first three national championships. She was a four-time all-American and was the school's all-time leading scorer—male or female.

But back in 1985 she was off to a rocky start. Randy Moore said in *Hoop Tales: Tennessee Lady Volunteers*, Summitt screamed "No!" into her telephone after a coaching friend called and told her of Gordon's apparent change of heart.

What was going on with Gordon that she would risk the wrath of Summitt? Years later she told Moore, "I probably committed to everybody who talked to me. At that point in time, I felt like it was a crime to say no, so I always said yes."

After Summitt cooled down some, she made a phone call and issued a cold, hard ultimatum to Gordon: "You give me a solid commitment or I give your scholarship to someone else." Gordon decided her commitment to Florida was a bad idea, and the rest is storied basketball history.

That surefire investment you made from a pal's hot stock tip. The expensive exercise machine. Blond hair. Telling your wife you wanted to eat at the restaurant with the waitresses in little shorts. They seemed like pretty good ideas at the time.

Long ago a man had what must have seemed like a good idea at the time. Turned out it wasn't. Judas's betrayal of Jesus remains one of the most heinous acts of treachery in history. Turning his back on Jesus was a bad idea for Judas then; it's a bad idea for you now.

> *Bat Day seems like a good idea, but I question the advisability of giving bats in the Bronx to 40,000 Yankee fans.*
> —Cartoonist Aaron Bacall

> **We all have some pretty bad ideas during our lifetimes, but nothing equals the folly of turning away from Jesus.**

Jumping for Joy

Read Luke 6:20–26.

"Rejoice in that day and leap for joy, for surely your reward is great in heaven" (v. 23).

One of UT's greatest jumpers is probably remembered more for his kicking. Karl Kremser lettered in football in 1967 and 1968, and his field goal with only fifty-nine seconds left—one of ten he kicked that season—propelled the Vols to a 17–14 win over LSU in 1967.

Kremser took a circuitous route to Knoxville and both gridiron and track acclaim. According to Haywood Harris and Gus Manning in *Six Seasons Remembered*, Ben Byrd of the *Knoxville Journal* called Kremser "the greatest thing to come out of Germany since Marlene Dietrich."

Kremser actually came to Knoxville because of UT's track program. "At West Point I was probably the worst cadet in the history of the academy," he told Harris and Manning. "Then I heard about Tennessee's track program, and with high jumping my second love and hearing about Richmond Flowers, I decided that was the place for me."

As things turned out, Knoxville was the place for Kremser.

Someone suggested he give football a try, and he did. "I felt like the kid in the candy store, getting to come to Tennessee as a walk-on kicker after playing soccer," he said. Perhaps his greatest thrill, though, came when he finished second in the high jump in the NCAA championships. He was first and foremost a jumper.

You're probably a pretty good jumper yourself when Tennessee scores against Alabama, Georgia, or Florida. You just can't help it. It's like your feet and your seat have suddenly become magnets that repel each other. The sad part is that you always come back down to earth: The moment of exultation passes.

But what if you could jump for joy all the time? Not literally, of course; you'd pass out from exhaustion. But figuratively, with your heart aglow and joyous even when life is most difficult. That's the way you are to live, Jesus said: always jumping for joy.

I would have thought that the knowledge that you are going to be leapt upon by half-a-dozen congratulatory, but sweaty teammates would be inducement not to score a goal.
—Broadcaster Arthur Marshall

≫ **Unbridled joy can send you jumping all over the place; Jesus said such exultation should not be something rare but a way of life.**

A Bolt Out of the Blue

Read Job 37.

"Listen, listen to the thunder of his voice. . . . Under the whole heaven he lets it loose, and his lightning to the corners of the earth" (vv. 2–3).

In 1952 Tennessee couldn't find a running back. The problem was so obvious and so acute that, according to Al Browning in *Third Saturday in October,* Tom Siler of the *Knoxville News-Sentinel* spoke of the "Tailback Blues" as being a hit song in East Tennessee.

So when the Vols hosted undefeated Alabama on October 18, nobody expected Tennessee to be able to run on the vaunted Tide—least of all with a tailback named Jimmy Wade. Wade, a sophomore, had never been in on a single play. He had not played at all in the 1952 season because of a knee injury, and he had spent his freshman season as a sub on defense.

He made his debut against Alabama, and it was a story for the ages. Siler wrote that Wade's "debut was unprecedented in the annals of Neyland football at Tennessee." He scored a touchdown and romped for 153 yards on eighteen carries to pace a 20–0 stomping of the Tide.

"Hey, who . . . was that guy?" Browning said a stunned Alabama player asked after the game. "We knew about [fullback Andy] Kozar, but nobody told us about the little guy." Alabama never saw this lightning bolt coming.

The unexpected is "a bolt out of the blue." Good, like Jimmy Wade's game against Alabama; or bad, like a letter from the IRS. "A bolt out of the blue" speaks of the unpredictability of life, the power of a lightning bolt, and the workings of a divine presence.

The thunderbolt is often associated with God. Your insurance company classifies a lightning strike as "an act of God," conceding God's command of the thunderbolt.

How wonderful it is that with all that power at his disposal, God restrains it, acting toward you with gentleness and love.

There's one word that describes baseball—"You never know."
—YOGI BERRA

⯈ **The awesome power of lightning pales beside God's power to control it, and yet God acts toward you with gentleness and love.**

Language Barrier

Read Acts 2:1–21.

"Divided tongues, as of fire, appeared among them, and a tongue rested on each of them. All of them were filled with the Holy Spirit and began to speak in other languages, as the Spirit gave them ability" (vv. 3–4).

In her early days in America, Violeta Retamoza let her golf do the talking.

A native of Aguascalientes, Mexico, Retamoza moved to Arizona, where she found her greatest challenge wasn't on the golf course. "It was a big change for me coming from Mexico," she told Austin Ward of the *Daily Beacon* in "Retamoza's Success." "It has been very hard." Her difficulties were compounded because when she started high school in America, she didn't speak a word of English.

Her English was better by the time she came to Knoxville in the fall of 2002. "When [Retamoza] was a freshman, we would tease her a little bit about her accent," coach Judi Pavon told Ward. "But her English has gotten better and better."

While her English may have caused her problems, there was nothing wrong with Retamoza's game. At Tennessee she was both all-SEC and all-American. She was the SEC Freshman of the Year and the first UT freshman golfer in history to be named second-team all-American. As a junior in 2004–05 she was named both the SEC Golfer of the Year and the SEC Scholar-Athlete of the Year. She set a school record for collegiate tournament wins. As Ward put it, "Her scores have never needed any translation."

Games translate easily across national and cultural boundaries, but language often erects a real barrier to understanding. Think of your vacation to Paris or Rome or Rio. Your call to a tech-support number about a computer problem, when you got someone who spoke English but didn't understand it. Your fender bender with a guy whose English was limited. You've learned one of life's lessons: Talking loud and waving your hands doesn't facilitate communication.

The message of faith is universal though, for people everywhere seek hope, purpose, and meaning in their lives. Nobody speaks that language better than Jesus.

Kindness is the universal language
that all people understand.
—LEGENDARY FLORIDA A&M COACH JAKE GAITHER

> *Jesus speaks across all language barriers because his message of hope and meaning resounds with people everywhere.*

Out of Character

Read Mark 6:1–6.

"'Is not this the carpenter, the son of Mary and brother of James and Joses and Judas and Simon, and are not his sisters here with us?' And they took offense at him" (v. 3).

Russ Bebb wrote in *The Big Orange* that the 1939 Orange Bowl against Oklahoma was considered "the roughest bowl game ever played" and that "a more fitting name would have been the 'Orange Brawl.'"

Tennessee won 17–0 to complete an 11-0 season, the first of three straight undefeated regular seasons. Tennessee great George Cafego "set the game's tempo on the very first play, knocking [Oklahoma's Waddy] Young head-over-heels with a vicious block." After that the "game settled down into a series of mini-brawls, with elbows and fists flying on almost every play."

At one point coach Bob Neyland "noticed that center Jim Rike was involved in more than his share of roughness." What the team needed was a peacemaker. So the coach called on backup Joe Little, instructing him to "get in there and get those guys together and settle them down." Little lasted only one play. After he snapped the ball, he was hit by a cheap shot, a vicious uppercut. The would-be peacemaker followed his assailant "downfield, returned the favor, then stood over the fallen Sooner while daring him to get up." He was promptly ejected from the game.

This was out of character for Little, who left the field apologizing to his coach.

You don't have to deck somebody as Little did, but people who know you are likewise surprised when you do something unexpected, like buying a flashy new car, getting your hair cut short or changing the color altogether, or suddenly changing jobs. Maybe even invigorating or discovering your faith life.

Acting out of character is the most telling mark of a person newly serious about or finding his or her faith. That character change reveals itself in a life centered on others, not yourself.

It can be a good thing not to act like yourself anymore—if you act like Jesus.

> *Sports do not build character. They reveal it.*
> —JOHN WOODEN

> **To be serious about Jesus is to act out of character:**
> **Rather than acting like yourself, you act like him.**

Doing What You've Gotta Do

Read 2 Samuel 12:1–15.

"The LORD sent Nathan to David" (v. 1).

The athletic directors at some schools carefully load their football schedules with a cupcake or two. The Tennessee Volunteers of modern times have certainly never ascribed to that theory. As often as not, the Vols' nonconference schedule includes at least one traditional powerhouse, such as Miami or Notre Dame.

But that wasn't the case back in the early 1920s, when Tennessee fans were clamoring for an upgrade of the schedule, according to Ward Gossett in *Volunteers Handbook.* The 1922 schedule had included such opponents as Emory-Henry, Carson-Newman, and Camp Benning. Even this was an upgrade from the 1905 schedule, which included the Tennessee School for the Deaf; in 1912 the Vols played the UT Medical School.

Powerhouse Army wanted a game in 1923, which coach M. Beal Banks earnestly tried to avoid, according to Gossett. UT officials said they would play, but only if they were guaranteed five thousand dollars, a sum they were sure Army would refuse. But the West Pointers didn't, and so the 1923 season began against Army.

Coach Banks didn't want to play that game, but a string of events that resulted in a signed contract hemmed him in. He had to do what he had to do, even when he didn't want to do it. (Somebody should have listened to him; Army won 41–0.)

You've had to do some things you didn't want to do. Maybe when you put your daughter on severe restriction, broke the news of a death in the family, fired a friend, or underwent surgery. You plowed ahead as best you could because you knew it was for the best or you had no choice.

Nathan surely didn't want to confront King David and tell him what a miserable reprobate he'd been, but the prophet had no choice: Obedience to God overrode all other factors. Obedience to God is not just for when God's wishes match our own, but for all the time.

> *Coaching is making men do what they don't want, so they can become what they want to be.*
> —TOM LANDRY

> **You can never foresee what God will demand of you, but obedience requires being ready to do whatever God asks.**

A Frustrating Season

Read Exodus 32:1–20.

"Moses' anger burned hot, and he threw the tablets from his hands and broke them at the foot of the mountain"
(v. 19).

How can one of the greatest seasons in Tennessee football history be frustrating?

In 1950 the Vols went 10-1 in the regular season, losing only to Mississippi State 7–0 the second week of the season in a shocking upset. They finished the season ranked number four in the nation. Then they scored two fourth-quarter touchdowns to rally and beat the heavily favored Texas Longhorns 20–14 in the Cotton Bowl.

That win, plus Army's 14–2 loss to Navy and Kentucky's 13–7 win over top-ranked Oklahoma in the Sugar Bowl (UT defeated Kentucky 7–0 that year), should have vaulted Tennessee to a national championship. One big problem frustrated the Vols, though, and they could do nothing about it: The season-ending polls were taken before the bowl games, even before the Army-Navy game.

Tailback Hank Lauricella, who had a classic seventy-five-yard touchdown run against Texas, voiced the Vols' frustration in Haywood Harris and Gus Manning's *Six Seasons Remembered:* "If the voting had been done after the bowls, we would have been first because Kentucky beat the number-one team, Oklahoma, in the Sugar Bowl." Sports fans "widely agreed that Tennessee's 20–14 win over Texas . . . would have vaulted the Vols into the number-one position if a post-bowl vote had been conducted." But there was no such poll.

The traffic light catches you when you're running late for work or your doctor's appointment. The bureaucrat gives you red tape when you want help. Your child refuses to take school-work seriously. Makes your blood boil, doesn't it?

Frustration is part of God's testing ground that is life. What's important is not that you encounter frustration—that's a given—but how you handle it. Do you respond with curses, screams, and violence? Or with a deep breath, a silent prayer, and calm persistence, even resolution when it's called for? Which way do you suppose God wishes you to respond?

A life of frustration is inevitable for any coach whose main enjoyment is winning.
—NFL HALL OF FAME COACH CHUCK NOLL

> **Frustration is a vexing part of life, but God expects us to handle it gracefully.**

The Sure Foundation

Read Luke 6:46–49.

"I will show you what someone is like who comes to me, hears my words, and acts on them. That one is like a man building a house, who dug deeply and laid the foundation on rock" (vv. 47–48).

You can't build anything solid and lasting unless there's a good foundation.

In his book *A Perfect Season,* coach Phillip Fulmer discussed laying the foundation for the 1998 national championship football team. Said the coach, "A championship team is not developed just from winter workouts, spring practice, or two-a-days: It is a process that takes years. The right mix includes quality recruiting, sound coaching, and good character in the young men that you bring into your program." As Fulmer put it, "We need character, not characters."

Of course, the Volunteers head coach could not know how everything would unfold in the fall of 1998, even as he saw that the winter workouts were exceptional. Preparing for that fateful season, though, Fulmer assessed the state of the Volunteer program and pronounced the foundation in place. "I knew we had talent, character, and sound coaching," he said.

In other words, the foundation necessary to consider seriously a run at the national championship had been laid, not just over a season but over years. An experienced, dedicated, and knowledgeable coaching staff had been assembled. Young men of both outstanding athletic ability and strong personal character had been recruited. Everything was in place and ready for success after years of preparation and building.

Your life is an ongoing project, a work in progress. Like any complex construction job, though, if your life is to be stable, it must have a solid foundation. Otherwise, like a football team that can't recover from a heartbreaking loss, your life heads downhill at the first trouble that comes your way.

R. Alan Culpepper commented in *The New Interpreter's Bible,* "We do not choose whether we will face severe storms in life; we only get to choose the foundation on which we will stand."

The one sure foundation is Jesus Christ.

> *First master the fundamentals.*
> —LARRY BIRD

> **In the building of your life, you must start with a good, solid foundation, or the first trouble that shows up will knock you down.**

The Winning Formula

Read 1 John 1:5–10.

"If we confess our sins, he who is faithful and just will forgive us our sins and cleanse us from all unrighteousness" (v. 9).

Pat Summitt is the most successful head coach in college basketball history.

On March 22, 2005, she became the winningest coach in NCAA basketball history—man or woman—with all of her wins coming at Tennessee. The 75–54 win over Purdue in the second round of the NCAA Tournament was her 880th, which carried her past the University of North Carolina's legendary Dean Smith. She was not only the first woman in NCAA Division I to win eight hundred games, but she achieved the eight-hundred-victory plateau faster than any coach in history, man or woman. She has already been inducted into the Basketball Hall of Fame and was named the Naismith Coach of the Century in April 2000.

Summitt roared past the nine-hundred-win mark during the 2005–6 campaign and will, in all likelihood, set a record for wins as a head coach that will never be broken. She won her unprecedented seventh national championship in 2007. Such unparalleled success must surely require at least a notebook full of what she expects from her players and the way they are to behave.

Not so.

"Sign here, go to class, play hard, don't embarrass the program, get a degree."

According to Marvin West in *Tales of the Tennessee Vols,* that's the simple, straightforward formula Summitt uses to explain to her players how she wants them to conduct themselves at UT.

Perhaps the simple life in America was doomed by the arrival of the programmable VCR. Since then we've pretty much been on an inevitably downward spiral into ever-more-complicated lives. But life itself, like basketball Pat Summitt–style, is best approached with the keen awareness that success requires simplicity, a sticking to the basics: Revere God, love your family, honor your country, do your best.

You're in good company. Theologians may make what God did in Jesus as complicated as quantum mechanics, but God kept it simple for you: Believe, trust, and obey. That's the true winning formula.

Golf is deceptively simple and endlessly complicated; it satisfies the soul and frustrates the intellect . . . [and is] the greatest game mankind has ever invented.
—ARNOLD PALMER

> **Life seems to get ever more complicated, but God gives simple directions: Believe, trust, and obey.**

Mamas and Their Children

Read John 19:25–30.

"Meanwhile, standing near the cross of Jesus [was] his mother" (v. 25).

T he Volunteers wound up with one of their greatest football players in history because his mama didn't like seeing her boy unhappy.

Stanley Morgan committed to Tennessee, but then word came that he had changed his mind and opted for South Carolina. Recruiting coordinator Sid Hatfield and coach Clifton Stewart hurried to the Morgan home, and Marvin West recounted what happened in *Tales of the Tennessee Vols*: "When [the coaches] got to the little frame house with the old Plymouth in the yard, the Morgans were gone. Neighbors said Stanley's mother had a new job, a new car and a new place to live."

The coaches located the Morgans, and "Stanley's mom confirmed that her new 'opportunities' were related to her son's decision to sign with South Carolina." The game was apparently up.

But a few days later Hatfield got a surprise phone call from

Stanley's mother. She told him she had quit the new job and had given up the new house and the new car. Then she asked if Tennessee still had a scholarship for her son.

Why had she given up all that stuff? Because, she said, "She hadn't seen her son smile once since she had made him switch to South Carolina." Above all else, Stanley Morgan's mama wanted her son happy.

Mamas do that sort of thing. Perhaps you can recall a time when your mother gave up something for you. Jesus's mother, too, would do anything for her son, including following him to his execution—an act of love and bravery, since her boy was condemned as an enemy of the Roman Empire. But just as Mary, your mom, and Stanley Morgan's mom would do anything for their children, so will God apparently do anything out of love for his children. After all, that was God on the cross where Mary stood, and he was dying for you.

Everyone should find time to write and to go see their mother. I think that's healthy.
—BEAR BRYANT

>> **Mamas often sacrifice for their children, but God, too, will do anything out of love for his children, including dying on a cross.**

Getting Ready

Read Luke 12:35–40.

"You also must be ready, for the Son of Man is coming at an unexpected hour" (v. 40).

owing might seem to be a sport in which team members show up for the fall season and work their way into shape. But that's not the way the Lady Vols approach their sport. The 2003–4 team was the most successful in Tennessee history, with a top-ten finish in the NCAA championships. To top that success, the Lady Vols turned to more intense preparation before the season started.

Chelsea Pemberton, a three-time all-American, explained to Jesse Morton of the *Daily Beacon* in "Lady Vol Rowing Team" that to get ready for the 2004–5 season, seven of the girls came back to Knoxville and trained during the summer. This was a change in routine. "Last summer everybody went home," Pemberton said. This particular summer, though, the team's "workouts tended to be more intense," according to Pemberton. "We were going on the water twice a day every day and on Tuesday and Thursday our morning water workout [was] replaced by lifting weights."

The result was a return to the NCAA championships for the Tennessee rowing team and a finish in the top eight nationally. Rowing is not simply a fall sport but rather a year-round endeavor. UT's rowers now stay ready all the time because, as Pemberton told Morton, "Rowing is an endurance sport."

Life, too, is an endurance sport, and you're in it for the long haul. So you schedule a physical, check your blood pressure at the supermarket pharmacy, walk or jog, and hop on the treadmill that doubles as a coat rack.

You also need to be concerned about your spiritual conditioning, which requires its own regimen. Jesus urged his team to be ready and dressed for action, to be in peak spiritual condition.

If UT's rowers aren't ready when the fall season begins, they lose a match. If you aren't ready when Jesus comes calling, you lose eternity.

> *Proper conditioning is that fleeting moment*
> *between getting ready and going stale.*
> —ALABAMA COACH FRANK THOMAS

Physical conditioning is good, but you also need to be in peak spiritual shape.

The Scars

Read Luke 24:36–43.

"Look at my hands and my feet; see that it is I myself"
(v. 39).

Bubba Wyche established himself as a Tennessee legend in 1967 when, as a junior, he made the first start of his career in Birmingham and quarterbacked the Volunteers to a stunning 24–13 win over Alabama. In the process UT snapped Bama's twenty-five-game winning streak, and Wyche became an overnight star.

Wyche had paid his dues. He lost his senior year in high school because of knee surgery. As Chris Cawood wrote in *Legacy of the Swamp Rat,* "Just as [Wyche] thought he had put his knee injury behind him, it buckled on him again two weeks into [UT's] spring practice of 1965." He had a second surgery on his left knee and lost another season.

Cawood wrote that by 1994, "Wyche's knees had been operated on nine times—seven on the left and two on the right. He underwent knee joint replacements in both knees in 1993." A staph infection set in, and Wyche underwent more surgery. "He woke up kneeless on the left side but thankful he had a leg and a life," Cawood said. His left leg wound up shorter than his right.

After his playing days, Bubba Wyche bore the scars of the game he was called to play.

You've got scars, too. That car wreck left a good one. So did that bicycle crash. Maybe we'd better not talk about the time you said, "Hey, watch this!" Your scars are part of your story.

People's scars are so unique that they're used to identify bodies. Even Jesus proved who he was by his scars. Why would he even have them in the first place? Why would he, who had all the power in the universe, submit meekly to being tortured and slaughtered?

He did it for you. Jesus bears the scars of his love for you.

*Andre Dawson has a bruised knee
and is listed as day-to-day. Aren't we all?*
—ANNOUNCER VIN SCULLY

⯈ **In your scars lie stories. The same is true for Jesus, whose scars tell of his love for you.**

A Matter of Perspective

Read John 20:11–18.

"Mary stood weeping outside the tomb" (v. 11).

One of the greatest plays in Tennessee football history may not have happened at all. It's a matter of perspective.

On November 7, 1959, a Volunteer team on its way to a 5-4-1 record pulled off one of college football's greatest upsets by stunning the defending national champion LSU Tigers 14–13 in Knoxville. The Tigers had Heisman-winner Billy Cannon and a nineteen-game win streak.

A Tennessee fumble at the Vol two-yard line late in the game let LSU pull within one at 14–13. The Tigers went for two on the conversion, and everybody in America knew what was coming. It came. Cannon got the ball and headed off his right tackle. Russ Bebb said in *The Big Orange,* "Wayne Grubb and Charley Severance hit him head-on, but Cannon kept chugging toward the goal just two feet away. Finally [Bill] Majors came roaring in to apply the clincher, and Cannon was stopped just inches short."

Or was he? According to Bebb, Cannon said, "I will go to my grave believing I was over."

"He wasn't," Severance declared in Marvin West's *Tales of the Tennessee Vols*. "Believe me, I was right there, and I know where the goal was."

Was the legendary stop made? It was all a matter of perspective, though the official's perspective was the one that stood.

Three of life's truths: If it feels good or tastes good, it's probably bad for you; lettuce is really clumpy grass; everyone will die. That last one is tougher to swallow than lettuce. (See Truth Number Two.) You can't avoid death, but you can face it from a perspective of fear or of hope.

Is it fearful, dark, fraught with peril and uncertainty? Or is it a passageway to glory, the light, and loved ones—an elevator ride to paradise? It's a matter of perspective that depends totally on whether you're standing by Jesus's side.

For some people it's the end of the rainbow,
but for us it is the end of the finish line.
—ROWER LARISA HEALY

> **Whether death is your worst enemy or a solicitous chauffeur is a matter of perspective.**

No Turning Back

Read Colossians 3:5–17.

"You have stripped off the old self with its practices and have clothed yourselves with the new self" (vv. 9–10).

Tyler DeVault left home to come to Tennessee and run cross country. When he left, he knew he couldn't go home again.

Well, if he wanted to run cross country, he couldn't.

DeVault became a Volunteer in the fall of 2004 expressly for the purpose of running cross country. A native of West Virginia, he originally stayed home by signing with the University of West Virginia. At the end of his freshman season, though, the program was eliminated. DeVault had to make some decisions: Would he stay at West Virginia and, as a result, give up cross country? If not, then to what college would he transfer?

As it turned out, the choices were easy enough. DeVault loved track too much to give it up unless injuries forced him to. And deciding where to run was easy. "The SEC is the best track conference in the nation," DeVault told David Klein of the *Daily Beacon* in "Cross Country Preview." "I leaped at the chance to run for the Volunteers" and coach George Watts.

So Tyler DeVault ran himself right into a new home, one

quite a distance from his native state, with new people, new traditions, and new customs. His former college life was gone forever, and new adventures lay ahead.

A new job, a new home, better schools for the kids—you'll load up a U-Haul or the back of a pickup and head out to a new place for any number of reasons. You leave the old behind and embrace the new, knowing you can never go back—and not wanting to.

Jesus brings a similar change to a person's life. Old ways are left behind; new habits beckon. With your eyes and your heart fixed on the road ahead, you set out for bigger and better days.

> *Don't live on the fading memories of your forefathers.*
> *Go out and make your own records, and leave some*
> *memories for others to live by.*
> —LEGENDARY VANDERBILT COACH DAN MCGUGIN

> **An encounter with Jesus Christ sets a life on a new road to adventure.**

A Distant Country

Read Luke 15:11–24.

"The father said to his slaves, 'Quickly, bring out a robe—
the best one—and put it on him; put a ring on his finger
and sandals on his feet. And get the fatted calf and kill it,
and let us eat and celebrate; for this son of mine was dead
and is alive again'" (vv. 22–24).

George Cafego, an all-American tailback at Tennessee in 1938 and 1939 and later an assistant coach, despised Vanderbilt so much he was willing to end a friendship with a colleague who flirted with taking a job with the Commodores.

Marvin West explained in *Tales of the Tennessee Vols* that the Volunteer legend hated the Commodores beyond reason or discussion. West said, "The mere mention of those stuffy, stilted elitists with their silver spoons caused Cafego to break out in a rash."

In the early 1970s Cafego and backfield coach Jim Wright shared office space. West said, "They were very good friends until Wright heard that the Commodores were looking for a new head coach and made the dreadful mistake of applying." Cafego refused even to speak to his "former" friend. West wrote, "It was impossible, as George saw it, for a Tennessee man to even consider consorting with Commodores." Cafego's response to what he saw as "betrayal, treason, a sad sellout" was "an icy stare and total silence."

Cafego considered Wright a traitor and a prodigal, a person who should never have even considered leaving home for a place he had no business being.

Maybe your children hang out with kids you don't particularly like. Your mother joins a motorcycle club. The Vols lose a key SEC game. Vexing, isn't it? But you can't control the people you love. You can throw them out of your life like so much garbage, or you can continue to love them and help them do their best. You can shut your heart to them, in effect sending them to a distant country, or you can keep your heart and your arms always open to keep them close.

So it is, too, in your relationship with God. You can shut your heart to him or open it. But either way, he'll be waiting for you with open arms.

By the way, Jim Wright didn't get the job, and Cafego relented with a gruff, "Welcome back, Jim."

> *You have no control over what the other guy does.*
> *You only have control over what you do.*
> —World Cup skier A. J. Kitt

> **You can't control the people you love, so you have a choice: Love them in spite of what they do, or drive them away.**

Family Men

Read Mark 3:31–35.

"He said, 'Here are my mother and my brothers! Whoever does the will of God is my brother and sister and mother'" *(vv. 34–35).*

"Tennessee's First Football Family"—the Majors family—was feted during a nationally televised win over Penn State in 1971. The occasion was Bobby Majors Day, and Russ Bebb said in *The Big Orange,* "The super safety closed out the Majors era at Knoxville with a stirring performance."

Bobby Majors was the last of the family to play for the Vols. Before him had come Johnny, an all-American and the third UT running back to gain at least a thousand yards in a season. He would eventually come back home to coach the Vols to a 116-62-8 record from 1977 to 1992. Then came Bill, perhaps best remembered as the sensational safety who was a part of one of the legendary plays in UT football history: the stop. He laid the clinching blow on Billy Cannon that kept him out of the end zone and preserved the stunning 14–13 win over LSU in 1959. Bill Majors was one of three UT assistant coaches killed in a train-car collision in 1965.

For the Majors clan, college football was truly a family affair. The players' storied history, particularly at UT, is the result of how their family life shaped and molded them. For the Majors boys, family is the essence of who and what they were and are.

Some wit said families are like fudge, mostly sweet with a few nuts. You can probably call the names of your sweetest relatives, whom you cherish, and of the nutty ones too. Like it or not, you have a family, and that's God's doing. God cherishes the family so much that he lived in one—and then redefined the family as all of his followers rather than as an accident of birth.

What a startling and wonderful thought: You have family members out there you don't even know, who stand ready to love you just because you're part of God's family.

Football has affected my entire family's lifestyle. My little boy can't go to bed unless we give him a two-minute warning.
—COACH DICK VERMEIL

For followers of Jesus, family comes not from a shared ancestry but from a shared faith.

Dry as a Bone

Read 1 Kings 16:29–17:1, 18:1.

"Elijah the Tishbite, of Tishbe in Gilead, said to Ahab, 'As the LORD the God of Israel lives, before whom I stand, there shall be neither dew nor rain these years, except by my word'" (v. 17:1).

The drought was of biblical proportions; it lasted eleven years.

On October 16, 1982, it ended in Knoxville when Tennessee came from eight points down in the last half to upset undefeated, second-ranked Alabama 35–28, ending eleven years of humility, frustration, and agony for Tennessee fans.

Early on it looked as though the drought would stretch into a dozen years when the Tide jumped out to a 14–3 lead. But Al Browning recounted in *Third Saturday in October* that Tennessee got back into the game when Alan Cockrell hit split end Willie Gault for a fifty-two-yard touchdown. Still, Alabama led 21–13 at halftime.

Tennessee took the lead for good in the second half when Cockrell passed thirty-nine yards to flanker Mike Miller to make it 24–21. When fullback Chuck Coleman broke open for a thirty-four-yard TD run, UT led 35–21 with 7:21 remaining.

Alabama rallied to score and then had three cracks at the end zone from the UT seventeen in the last minute. But defensive back Lee Jenkins leveled a Bama receiver in the end zone just as the ball arrived, and it popped into the waiting arms of defensive end Mike Terry to seal the win.

The drought was over.

You can walk across that river you went boating on in the spring. The city's put all neighborhoods on water restriction. As a result, that beautiful lawn you fertilized and seeded will turn a sickly, pale green and may lapse all the way to brown. Those jonquils probably won't bloom anymore either. Somebody wrote "Wash me" on the rear window of your truck.

The sun bakes everything, including the concrete. The earth itself seems exhausted, just barely hanging on. It's a drought.

It's the way a soul looks that shuts out God.

> *Drink before you are thirsty. Rest before you are tired.*
> —PAUL DE VIVIE, FATHER OF FRENCH CYCLE TOURING

> **Our souls thirst for the refreshing presence of God.**

The Heart of the Matter

Read 1 Samuel 13:1–14.

"The Lord has sought out a man after his own heart"
(v. 14).

When he was hired, his instructions were simple, if difficult: "Even the score with Vanderbilt."

According to Russ Bebb in *The Big Orange*, that's what Dean Nathan Dougherty told Bob Neyland when he hired him as head football coach in 1925. After all, Vandy was the big rival and had an 18-2-1 edge in the series. Bebb wrote, "Like a good soldier Neyland carried out the order," compiling a 16-3-2 record against the Commodores.

Over the years, though, as Neyland led Tennessee to fortune and fame on the football field, Vanderbilt was replaced—at least in Neyland's heart—as the measuring stick for the Vols. Whipping Alabama became more important for the legendary coach because he knew that to whip the Tide was to whip the best.

And Neyland knew something more. After all, according to Chris Warner's *SEC Sports Quotes,* the great coach once said, "You never know what a football player is made of until he plays Alabama." Neyland knew that beating Alabama required something more than talent and execution, important as they were.

Jim Haslam, a member of the 1951 national championship team that defeated Alabama 27–13, recalled to Al Browning in *Third Saturday in October*, "I remember the general pointing at his heart and saying, 'Here is where you beat Alabama.'" Beating Alabama required heart.

We all face defeat; even General Neyland lost some games. At some time you probably have admitted you were whipped, no matter how much it hurt to do so. Always in your life, though, you have known that you would fight for some things with all your heart and never give up: your family, your country, your friends, your core beliefs.

God should be on that list too. He seeks men and women who will never turn their backs on him, because they are people after God's own heart.

God's team is a mighty good one to be on, but it takes heart.

*It is not the size of a man but the size
of his heart that matters.*
—EVANDER HOLYFIELD

▸ **To be on God's team requires the heart of a champion.**

Tough Love

Read Mark 10:17–22.

"Jesus, looking at him, loved him and said, 'You lack one thing; go, sell what you own, and give the money to the poor, and you will have treasure in heaven; then come, follow me.' When he heard this, he was shocked and went away grieving" (vv. 21–22).

Pat Summitt once kicked an entire team out of the dressing room—for a month!

The legendary coach of the Lady Vols is known for her tough love. In his book *Tales of the Tennessee Vols,* Marvin West declared, "Rivals say Pat Summitt is the General George Patton of women's basketball." The incident with the dressing room, as West related it, underscores Summitt's tough approach to the game and to the women who play for her.

West said, "Tennessee's locker room is a beautiful place, a museum of championship trophies, All-America nameplates and classy fittings that go with winning." Back in 1990 the head Vol thought her team wasn't worthy of the grand surroundings that had been the home of so many champions. So she kicked the entire squad out of their sumptuous home, telling them, "Get out! You haven't paid the rent."

So the players obediently packed up their gear and moved down the hall. And what did their new digs look like? West said the players found themselves in "a spare room with cinder-block walls and metal folding chairs." It took the players a month to get out of the doghouse and back into the penthouse.

Strict with your kids? Expect them to abide by your rules? The immediate reward you receive may be an intense and loud "I hate you," a flounce, and a slammed door. So why do it? Because you're the parent; you love your children, and you want them to become responsible adults. It's tough love.

Jesus is tough on the ones he loves, too. That includes you. He expects you to do what he said—to do right. And a well-executed flounce won't change things. But you'll be better for it—and thankful for it—in the end.

The sterner the discipline, the greater the devotion.
—BASKETBALL COACH PETE CARILL

▶ *Jesus expects you to do what he has told you to do— but it's because he loves you and wants the best for you.*

Deserving Better

Read Isaiah 55:6–13.

"My thoughts are not your thoughts, nor are your ways my ways" (v. 8).

Jerry Colquitt deserved better.

Marvin West wrote in *Tales of the Tennessee Vols,* Colquitt had "quick feet" and a "keen mind" and "threatened to beat out Heath Shuler and win the quarterback job in the spring of '92."

But he didn't, and while Shuler went on to become part of Volunteer lore, Colquitt sat on the bench—for three years.

He didn't give up, though, sticking it out until his turn finally came in 1994. Head coach Phillip Fulmer named him the starting quarterback for the season opener against UCLA.

Seven plays into the season it was all over.

"It was third and seven when we called an option," Colquitt recalled to Tony Basilio in "Full Circle." "I tried to split [two defenders] when I felt something. . . . It was a torn ACL, an injury that ended up taking six months to fully recover from." On the first series, Colquitt's brief career ended with a knee injury.

West recorded Fulmer's comment that Colquitt's injury was "one of the saddest moments I've ever experienced in football. Jerry had worked so hard and paid a high price to get to play. That's not how it is supposed to end."

No, it isn't, but it did. It was just one of those things.

You've probably had a few of "those things" in your own life: bad breaks that occur without regard to justice, morality, or fair play. You wonder if everything in life is simply random, events determined by a chance roll of some cosmic dice. Can there really be a plan in all this? Is there really somebody at the helm?

Yes, there can be, and yes, there is. The plan belongs to God, the one in charge, who asks that you trust him, since he knows how everything will turn out—and that everything will be all right.

In sport, part of the game is accepting the umpire's call, no matter how hard that might be. Sometimes the calls go your way, and sometimes they don't.
—Olympic gold medalist Dot Richardson

> **Life unwinds as God wants it to, confounding us because—unlike God—we can't see the end of the story.**

DAY 74

Flat Busted

Read Luke 12:22–34.

"Strive for his kingdom, and these things will be given to you as well" (v. 31).

As the Tennessee athletic association entered the twentieth century, it was pretty much flat busted. Russ Bebb noted in *The Big Orange* that in 1899 the chairman of UT athletics complained that if the "university president, students, and faculty 'cannot be gotten to take an interest in this matter the committee will recommend that [football] be cut out.'"

Compared to today's budgets of millions of dollars, the money crunch UT suffered back then seems quaint—but it was real. Bebb quoted an appeal to Tennessee alumni in the *Knoxville Sentinel* in October 1899 that declared, "We need the funds for coaching, for outfitting the team, and for old outstanding debts."

Bebb recorded that the 1902 game against Vanderbilt lost $60.90, and the Sewanee game the same year lost $15.80, though Maryville drew enough fans to show a profit of $45.35.

The financial crunch didn't occur because the athletic association was wasting money. Bebb quoted a list of expenses from *The Volunteer State Forges Its University* that provides insight into football in another age: football pants $3.00 a pair; head pieces $1.35 each; sweaters (padded) $1.50 each; football $4.00; and whiskey $2.25. That last item is certainly a strange one, and Bebb noted that research never turned up exactly what the whiskey was used for.

Having a little too much money at the end of the month may be as bothersome—if not as worrisome—as having a little too much month at the end of the money. The investment possibilities are bewildering: stocks, bonds, mutual funds, 401(k), Roth IRA, that group pooling their money to open up a neighborhood coffee shop—that's a good idea. And how do they figure the Dow Jones Industrial Average?

You take your money seriously, as well you should. How much of it, though, are you investing with God?

An athlete cannot run with money in his pockets. He must run with hope in his heart and dreams in his head.
—Olympic champion Emil Zatopek

> **Your attitude about money says much about your attitude toward God.**

No Carrying Charge

Read Mark 2:1–12.

"Some people came, bringing to him a paralyzed man, carried by four of them" (v. 3).

Tennessee's irrepressible basketball coach Ray Mears once outsmarted an official and thus avoided a series of technical fouls that could have cost the Vols the game.

This particular confrontation occurred during a game at Ole Miss in the 1960s. As Randy Moore recounted in *Hoop Tales: Tennessee Volunteers Men's Basketball,* Mears "stormed onto the playing floor to confront" a referee after a call the coach thought was particularly egregious. Apparently the ref had had enough of Mears's badgering and fulminating. Moore said the ref nodded toward the Tennessee sidelines and "snapped, 'It's going to cost you one technical foul for each step it takes you to get back to the bench.'"

Moore said, "Mears's feet were still but his brain was going a hundred miles per hour. With a smug grin, he beckoned assistant coaches Stu Aberdeen and Sid Hatfield to pick him up and carry him back to the bench. . . . Mears never let his feet touch the ground on the return trip to the sidelines." Perhaps with a grin he managed to subdue, the outmaneuvered ref admitted to Mears, "OK, you got me that time," but he promised to "get" the coach if he came back onto the court again.

Sometime in your adult life, you've probably had to depend on the assistance of others. You may have had the flu or arthroscopic knee surgery or a broken bone that laid you up. You've needed somebody to carry you, even if only for a short while.

But you can develop weak spots spiritually as well as physically. Then it's not a case of being physically unable to do something; rather, it's doing what you know is wrong or not doing what you know is right. Then, too, you need to turn to someone for help and healing.

Jesus is the one.

I do not participate in any sport
with ambulances at the bottom of a hill.
—ERMA BOMBECK

⯈ **Friends and family may help us heal up physically;**
Jesus tends to our spiritual healing.

Answering the Call

Read 1 Samuel 3:1–18.

"The LORD came and stood there, calling as before, 'Samuel! Samuel!' And Samuel said, 'Speak, for your servant is listening'" (v. 10).

G reatness in any team sport requires players to answer the call the coaches put upon them and to do whatever is necessary to help the team, even if it means putting aside personal goals and desires. In the spring of 2005, freshman Joselyn Johnson answered the call for the UT volleyball team.

Austin Ward of the *Daily Beacon* explained in "Johnson Looks to Replace Piantadosi" that Johnson was a middle blocker for the Lady Vols as a freshman. When all-SEC and honorable mention all-American outside hitter Michelle Piantadosi graduated, coach Rob Patrick was faced with a huge hole in his otherwise experienced team. He turned to Johnson, now a talented rising sophomore, and called on her to make the position change.

Patrick understood that the change wasn't an easy one for Johnson. One reason was that she was what the coach called "a great player in the middle. She's comfortable in the middle and she knows that position, and all of a sudden she goes to an outside hitter position where she doesn't have that comfort level."

But Johnson did what the coach asked. "Her attitude has been incredibly great," Patrick said. "She's taking our coaching well and really trying to do the things that we're asking her to do."

In the best tradition of UT athletes, Joselyn Johnson answered the call.

What's the call for your life? Zambia? Cleveland? A minister?

Talk about scary.

You hear about God's "calling someone," telling someone what to do with his or her life. That means one thing, right? Moving the family halfway around the world to a place where the folks have never heard of air-conditioning, baseball, or paved roads—and being a minister of some sort.

Not for you, no thank you. And who can blame you?

But God usually calls folks to serve him where they are. In fact, God put you where you are right now. Are you serving him there?

It was like being in a foreign country.
—WELSH SOCCER PLAYER IAN RUSH ON PLAYING IN ITALY

> **Serving God doesn't necessarily mean entering full-time ministry and going to a foreign land; God calls you to serve him right where you are.**

Ten to Remember

Read Exodus 20:1–17.

*"God spoke all these words: 'I am the Lord your
God . . . you shall have no other gods before me'"
(vv. 1–3).*

In *The Big Orange,* Russ Bebb listed Tennessee's ten biggest
football wins in terms of margin of victory. All ten romps occurred in the period from 1905 to 1951. The only games of
more recent times to threaten to make the slaughter list are
the 70–3 win over Louisiana Monroe in 2000 and the 1994
65–0 romp over Vanderbilt.

The greatest point spread of all in Tennessee's long and storied gridiron history occurred way back in 1905, when the Vols
annihilated American University 104–0. Bebb said the *Knoxville Journal* expected the blowout, noting in its pregame article, "Victory for the Orange and White is sure, as certain as if
the contest were over and the result announced."

The trouncing of American wasn't the only time Tennessee
reached the century mark. Three times the Vols won by a score
of 101–0: in 1912 against King and twice in 1915 against
Carson-Newman and Cumberland.

The rest of the top ten, in order of margin, are 95–0 against Athens in 1915 (not the University of Georgia), 89–0 over Carson-Newman in 1914, an 80–0 rout of Kentucky Central in 1915, 75–0 over Maryville in 1913, 73–0 against Carson-Newman in 1929, and a 68–0 romp over Tennessee Tech in 1951.

For Tennessee fans, these are indeed ten to remember for the ages.

Lists are great. When you've got your list, you're ready to go: a gallon of paint and a water hose from the hardware store; chips, peanuts, and sodas from the grocery store for tonight's neighborhood meeting; the dry cleaning; tickets for the band concert. Your list helps you remember.

God once made a list of things he wanted you to remember: the Ten Commandments. Just as your list reminds you to do something, so God's list reminds you of how you are to act in your dealings with other people and with him.

Society today treats the Ten Commandments as if they were the ten suggestions. Never compromise on right or wrong.
—COLLEGE BASEBALL COACH GORDIE GILLESPIE

God's list is a set of instructions on how you are to conduct yourself with other people and with him.

Top Secret

Read Romans 2:1–16.

"Their conflicting thoughts will accuse or perhaps excuse them on the day when, according to my gospel, God, through Jesus Christ, will judge the secret thoughts of all" *(vv. 15–16).*

Legendary UT football coach Bob Neyland suffered from "spy-phobia."

At least that's the opinion of Russ Bebb, who wrote of Neyland's obsession with secrecy in *The Big Orange*. For Neyland, "spy-phobia" took a particular form. He was constantly afraid "that someone was spying on his practice sessions from atop Cherokee Bluffs, a broad-faced cliff . . . that held a commanding view of the Vols' practice field."

Gus Manning was Neyland's "sports publicity director, trouble-shooter, watchdog, and general handyman—and one of his closest associates." He told Bebb that he made many a spy run up to Cherokee Bluffs to hunt for anyone with a pair of binoculars. "I never did find anybody with binoculars, but I once ran into the same two lovers up there about four times in one week," Manning recalled. "It was pretty embarrassing. I'd go back and tell the general each time, and he just couldn't get over it. . . . 'The same ones?' he'd ask."

Strangers in the stands also disconcerted the secretive coach. When the Vols had a closed practice at the stadium, Neyland would want to know everyone who was sitting in the stands. "I'd have to be able to tell him," Manning said. "I don't think we ever did run across anybody spying, though."

As Bob Neyland was about his football practices, you have to be vigilant about the personal information you prefer to keep secret. In our information age, a lot of data about you— from credit reports to what movies you rent—is readily available. People you don't know may know a lot about you—or at least they can find out. And some of them may use that information for harm.

That's why it's especially comforting to know that God, the one before whom you have no secrets, is not your enemy but is on your side.

> *I believe in God. He is the secret of my success.*
> —ALGERIAN OLYMPIAN NOUREDDINE MORCELI

> **We have no secrets before God; good thing he's on our side.**

A Lesser Court

Read Mark 8:31–38.

*"He began to tell them that the Son of Man must un-
dergo great suffering, and be rejected by the elders, the
chief priests, and the scribes, and be killed" (v. 31).*

When the Lady Vols basketball program was resurrected
in 1960 after a thirty-four-year hiatus, the team didn't get a lot
of respect.

During a game at Carson-Newman College, the teams were
told at halftime that they could not finish the game on the
main gym floor because the men's team was to use the gym
for its pregame warm-ups. Coach Nancy Lay told Randy Moore
in *Hoop Tales: Tennessee Lady Volunteers* that the women's teams
were thus banished to the basement of the building and "a
lesser court."

Lay recalled, "There was a track above the gym where we
played the second half. One time the ball was passed to Brenda
Green, and I yelled for her to shoot. When she did, the ball hit
the underside of the track, then came down and hit Brenda in
the head, knocking her out cold."

In those early days the program didn't garner much respect, even among the students and the potential players. "Some of the better players preferred intramurals because they were in sororities and didn't want to spend the extra time it would take to practice for the varsity," Lay remembered. The school administration also didn't give the team much respect—or money. Lay's players paid their own transportation costs and the tournament entry fees.

Rodney Dangerfield made a good living as a comedian with a repertoire that was really only countless variations on one punch line: "I don't get no respect." Dangerfield was successful because he struck a chord with his audience. No one wants to be perceived as being worthy of only "a lesser court." You want the respect, honor, esteem, and regard that you feel you've earned.

Probably more often than not, you don't get it, but that doesn't stop you from succeeding. Anyway, don't feel too bad; you're in good company. Look how they treated Jesus.

> *Play for your own self-respect and the respect of your teammates.*
> —Vanderbilt coach Dan McGugin

> **You may not get the respect you deserve, but dare to succeed anyway.**

Expecting the Unexpected

Read Luke 2:1–20.

"She gave birth to her firstborn son and wrapped him in bands of cloth, and laid him in a manger" (v. 7).

Tennessee used the unexpected to flabbergast and stun favored Alabama 25–0 in 1931.

Al Browning wrote in *Third Saturday in October* that coach Bob Neyland "shocked the Crimson Tide with his unusual game plan." And what was so totally unexpected that Alabama wound up "confused and battered" from what Browning called Neyland's "sneak attack"?

Tennessee threw the ball.

Teams rarely passed back then, not necessarily because they couldn't but because the ball didn't lend itself to passing. A Tennessee student of the era told Browning, "It's amazing anybody could throw a football back then. They were big, fat, bulky things."

The passer that wonderful October afternoon was as unexpected as the passes themselves. He was Tennessee's all-American halfback Gene McEver, a bullish runner not known—with good reason—for his passing ability. Browning quoted sportswriter Herbert Barrier: "In practice, Gene is likely to hit himself in the back of the head when he attempts to pass."

On this particular afternoon, though, McEver was, according to end Al Mark, "a sharpshooting fool." McEver didn't exactly fill the air with footballs by contemporary standards, but he was on target, hitting all six of the passes he attempted for eighty-eight yards.

It wasn't the rifle arm but the unexpectedness of the tosses that surprised the Tide and left them bamboozled and defeated.

Just like Alabama in 1931, we think we've got everything figured out and planned for, and then something unexpected happens. Someone gets ill; you fall in love; you lose your job; you're going to have another child. Life surprises us with its bizarre twists and turns.

God is that way too, catching us unawares to remind us he's still around. A friend who hears you're down and stops by, a child's laugh, an achingly beautiful sunset—unexpected moments of love and beauty. The most unexpected thing God ever did, though, was send Jesus to bring us closer to him. How will you respond?

Sport is about adapting to the unexpected and being able to modify plans at the last minute.
—SIR ROGER BANNISTER, FIRST-EVER SUB-FOUR-MINUTE MILER

> **God does the unexpected to remind us of his presence—like showing up as Jesus.**

Divided Loyalties

Read Matthew 6:24.

"No one can serve two masters" (v. 24).

While most families may agree on their loyalty to God and country, it may be another matter when college loyalties come into play. Many families find themselves with divided loyalties when Tennessee plays some of its fiercest rivals.

In *Tales of the Tennessee Vols,* Marvin West told of one such family, Wes and Jennifer Coffman. West said they first saw each other after the Tennessee-Kentucky basketball game in Lexington in 1966. Wes Coffman was a Volunteer guard; Jennifer Burcham was a Wildcat cheerleader. As West put it, they met "right out in front of God and everybody, on the court at Memorial Coliseum. Jennifer was smiling. Her team had won. Wes was able to muster a small smile. He didn't know that many cheerleaders."

When Kentucky came to Knoxville for the season finale, "Jennifer expected to see Wes, but he had another date." To his credit, West said, "Coffman, a Kentuckian not considered quick enough to play for the Big Blue, was quick enough to grasp the situation."

They started up a regular correspondence and eventually married, but they still pulled for their respective schools. The color of the hat—orange or blue—on their home's hat rack always reflected which team had won the most recent encounter. Theirs was a household with divided loyalties.

You probably understand the stress that comes with divided loyalties. The Christian work ethic drives you to be successful. The world, however, often makes demands and presents images that conflict with your devotion to God: Movies deride God; couples play musical beds in TV sitcoms; and TV dramas portray Christians as killers following God's orders.

Your desk is piled high with work; it's awfully quiet in the office on Sunday morning. What do you do when your heart and loyalties are pulled in two directions?

Keep your loyalty to God—always.

I am the most loyal player money can buy.
—DON SUTTON

> **God does not condemn you for being successful and enjoying popular culture, but your loyalty must lie first and foremost with him.**

Fear Factor

Read Matthew 14:22–33.

"They cried out in fear. But immediately Jesus spoke to them and said, 'Take heart, it is I; do not be afraid'"
(vv. 26–27).

Ricky Gregg must have seemed fearless to his Asian caddy.

Gregg, a former Volunteer golfer, played the Asian circuit in 1981 and 1982. His wife, Kim, a former majorette with the Pride of the Southland band, made the trip with him. As Marvin West recounted in *Tales of the Tennessee Vols,* Gregg had a little girl named Prim as his caddy for a tournament in Bangkok. He was told under no circumstances to pay her more than $1.50 a day, but nobody said anything about shopping. "She got some things she wanted, jeans and make-up," Gregg said. "That week, she was part of the family."

The weather for the Bangkok tournament was stifling, and Gregg walked in the shade at the edge of the rough as much as he could to escape the heat. To his dismay, however, little Prim remained in the fairways, tugging and lugging the heavy bag in the hot sun. Repeatedly Gregg signaled for her to join him, but she never did. Ricky and Kim "talked about whether Prim was afraid to walk with [Ricky] near the woods. Finally, we asked the caddy-master. He said she was scared.

"'That's where the cobras are.'"

Some fears are well merited; others are frightful only to us. Speaking to the Rotary Club calls for a heavy dose of antiperspirant. Elevator walls feel like they're closing in on you. And don't even get started on spiders and snakes.

We all live in fear, and God knows this. Dozens of passages in the Bible urge us not to be afraid. God isn't telling us to lose our wariness of oncoming cars, big dogs with nasty dispositions, or cobras crawling around on a golf course. He's reminding us that when we trust in him, we find peace that calms our fears.

> *Let me win. But if I cannot win,*
> *let me be brave in the attempt.*
> —SPECIAL OLYMPICS MOTTO

You have your own peculiar set of fears, but they need never paralyze you, because God is greater than anything you fear.

Peacemongers

Read Hebrews 12:14–17.

"Pursue peace with everyone, and the holiness without which no one will see the Lord" (v. 14).

Ron Widby remains a Tennessee legend to this day, the first UT athlete ever to make all-American in both football and basketball. He was a competitor but not a fighter. Except for one occasion when he landed a punch on a teammate's jaw.

In *Hoop Tales: Tennessee Volunteers Men's Basketball,* Randy Moore wrote that in 1967 the basketball coaches decided to make practices more physical in preparation for upcoming SEC games. They told the scout squad to use "roughhouse tactics." Moore said the scout teamers "enthusiastically grabbed, shoved, elbowed, and kneed the first teamers" while the coaches stood by and didn't call a single foul.

As one who knew about such things, Widby said, "It was tougher than a lot of football practices." Finally, the star had had enough, and he warned one of the freshmen to stop so much rough stuff. "He hit me again on the very next play," Widby said. "I turned around and decked him with one punch."

Widby said he expected to be chastised, and he braced himself for the chewing out he knew he deserved when assistant coach Stu Aberdeen came running up to him. To his surprise, Aberdeen exclaimed, "Ronnie, Ronnie, you mustn't do that. What if you broke your hand?"

Perhaps you've never been in a barroom brawl or a public brouhaha. But maybe, like Ron Widby, you retaliated when you got one elbow too many in a basketball game. Or maybe you and your spouse or your teenager get into it occasionally, shouting and saying cruel things. Or road rage may be a part of your life.

While we seem to live in a more belligerent, confrontational society than ever before, fighting is not the answer to a problem. Actively seeking and making peace is. It's not as easy as fighting, but it's a lot less painful.

No matter what the other fellow does on the field, don't let him lure you into a fight. Uphold your dignity.
—ALABAMA COACH FRANK THOMAS

▶ **Making peace instead of fighting takes courage and strength, but it's certainly the less painful option.**

Glory Days

Read Colossians 3:1–4.

"When Christ who is your life is revealed, then you also will be revealed with him in glory" (v. 4).

Many Volunteer fans today may not even know the name Johnny Butler. But during a 21–0 win over Alabama in 1939, Butler made what is arguably the greatest run in Tennessee football history.

In *Third Saturday in October,* Al Browning said Butler's jaunt was "a fifty-six-yard touchdown run about which people continue to marvel. He zigged and zagged, . . . breaking what seemed like a dozen tackles in the process, running what seemed like 120 yards, and secured legendary status." An Alabama player on the field that day conceded, "It was one of the more remarkable plays I have witnessed."

Alabama end Holt Rast said he hollered to tackle Fred Davis after Butler had come by him twice, "'Fred, I've had two shots at him and I haven't tackled him.' And Fred yelled, 'Don't worry about it, Holt, he'll be back around a third time.'"

Legendary sportscaster Lindsey Nelson told Browning "The Run" was seen by a whole lot of people because it was used repeatedly by movie folks. "Any time there was a need for a climax, a long run, a thrilling ending to a football game, the Johnny Butler run was used," Nelson said.

Thus did Johnny Butler find glory that day from one remarkable play.

You, too, may remember the play that was your moment of glory in athletics. Or the night you received an award from a civic group for your hard work. Your first (and last?) ace on the golf course. Your promotion at work. Your first-ever 10K race. Life does have its moments of glory.

But they amount to a lesser, transient glory, which actually carries pain with it, since you cannot recapture the moment. True glory days—which last forever—are found only through Jesus.

The real glory is being knocked to your knees and then coming back. That's real glory. That's the essence of it.
—VINCE LOMBARDI

▷ **The glory of this earth is fleeting, but the glory we find in Jesus lasts forever.**

The Middle of Nowhere

Read Genesis 28:10–22.

"Jacob woke from his sleep and said, 'Surely the LORD is in this place—and I did not know it!'" (v. 16)

Charlie Fulton came to Tennessee in the fall of 1964 as a highly recruited quarterback, a runner who could pass. In Knoxville, though, he was just one of seven hopefuls on the freshman team, a group that included Bubba Wyche and Dewey Warren.

Freshmen couldn't play on the varsity in those days, and when the season ended, all three knew they were in the hunt for the starting job in the fall of 1965. Chris Cawood wrote in *Legacy of the Swamp Rat,* "Fulton knew that his weaknesses were in the center exchange and familiarity with the varsity receivers. In the late spring and early summer of 1965 he remedied that."

Instead of going home when school was out, Fulton went to what he described as "the middle of nowhere." He joined a center and a receiver at a football camp in Tellico. The three Vols were ostensibly there as counselors, but when they had free time, they snapped and threw. After all, they didn't have anything else to do.

As a result of all that time spent "in the middle of nowhere" with those thousands of repetitions, Cawood said Fulton "came into fall practice as the one to beat for the quarterback job." And he won the job.

Ever been to Hornbeak? Lutts? Or Helenwood, just up the road from Robbins and Elgin? They are among the many villages that dot the Tennessee countryside. Miles from I-40 or anything else resembling a four-lane highway, they seem to be in the middle of nowhere, the type of place where Charlie Fulton trained for the UT quarterbacking job in 1965.

But God is in Middleton and Toone just as he is in Knoxville. Even when you are far from the roads well traveled, you are with God. The middle of nowhere is, in fact, holy ground—because God is there.

The middle of nowhere is the place that teaches you that crossing the goal line first is not as important as the course you took to get there.

—DIVE INSTRUCTOR RIDLON KIPHART

No matter how far off the beaten path you travel, you're still on holy ground, because God is there.

A Level Playing Field

Read Romans 3:21–26.

"There is no distinction, since all have sinned and fall short of the glory of God" (vv. 22–23).

Coach Zora Clevenger told Russ Bebb in *The Big Orange* about just how bad the Volunteer home football field was in the early years. UT's head coach from 1911 to 1915 said the field was so hard "that present-day players would refuse to use it."

The field was Wait Field, an open place with hard, packed dirt and a little bit of grass that disappeared early every fall. Gravel that washed onto the field from a hillside made the conditions even worse.

Gravel and hard dirt weren't the only problems with Wait Field. The north end zone ran smack up against an iron fence running along Cumberland Avenue so that, according to Bebb, "more than one pass receiver was a bit gun-shy as he went into that end zone after a pass."

The south end zone, however, was a receiver's dream because part of it was on a hill. UT receivers learned early on that "they could get atop the hill and haul in passes without the defensive backs being able to do much about it." Naturally, this led to some vehement protests, so "school officials marked off the field with a curved line running through the end zone." The part of the end zone that was elevated was beyond the line and was out of bounds.

Like old Wait Field, life's playing field isn't level either. Others, it seems, get all the breaks while you work yourself to exhaustion. It seems some people just have it made. Maybe, but look around carefully and you'll also see a veteran who lost his legs to a land mine, a schizophrenic woman living under an overpass, or a neighbor with kidney failure.

The only place in life where we really stand on a level playing field is before God. There, all people are equal because we all need the lifeline God offers through Jesus—and we all have access to it.

If you don't have the best of everything,
make the best of everything you have.
—COACH ERK RUSSELL

▶ **Unlike life's playing field, God's playing field is level, because everyone has equal access to what God has done through Jesus Christ.**

Suit Up

Read Ephesians 6:10–17.

*"Be strong in the Lord and in the strength of his power.
Put on the whole armor of God, so that you may be able
to stand against the wiles of the devil" (vv. 10–11).*

Accprding to TheGoal.com, when the Green Bay Packers
were seeking to sign Reggie White as a free agent, Packers
coach Mike Holmgren left a message on White's answering
machine that said, "Reggie, this is God. Go to Green Bay."

An ordained Baptist minister, the "Minister of Defense"
was a legend at Tennessee and in the NFL before he died at age
forty-three in December 2004. Twice he was the NFL Defensive Player of the Year, and he retired as the all-time sack
leader. At UT he set the school record for sacks, and in 1983,
his senior season, he was a unanimous all-American.

According to Marvin West in *Tales of the Tennessee Vols,*
White was perturbed that Tennessee assistant coach Jim Dyar
was missing his own son's high-school games to recruit him.
When White asked him how many times he had seen his son
play and Dyar answered none because his job was to see
Reggie and recruit him for Tennessee, White said, "I'm

coming to Tennessee, but I might change my mind if you don't stay home and see your son next Friday night."

Reggie White was a physically tough man whose profession demanded violence and confrontation, but he was also a spiritually tough man of God who practiced love and reconciliation.

You go to work and swim with the sharks, making an honest living in a world that rewards callousness, greed, and unbridled ambition. You raise your children in a world that glamorizes immoral behavior and ridicules values. You espouse decency in a world that spews garbage and hatred. It's tough being a person of faith and principle.

Standing tall for what you believe may get you admired, but it also makes you a target. You need protection like that which a football player has with his pads. And you have it—and more—in the strength and the power of almighty God.

As far as I'm concerned, being a Christian makes
you more of a man.
—Reggie White

▶ **God did not create you ten feet tall and bulletproof, so he arms you with his strength and his power.**

At a Loss

Read Philippians 3:7–11.

"I regard everything as loss because of the surpassing value of knowing Christ Jesus my Lord" (v. 8).

Not all the losses in any athletic program take place on the field or the court.

The 1965 football season got off to a great start. The Vols buried LSU 21–0 and South Carolina 24–3 and tied Auburn 13–13 and Alabama 7–7, the only blemish on the Tide's 9-0-1 record. The tie sparked a spirit of celebration in Knoxville, but it didn't last.

As Russ Bebb told it in *The Big Orange,* on the Monday morning following the Alabama game, three assistant coaches were killed when a Southern Railway train hit their car. Bob Jones and Bill Majors died instantly; Charlie Rash lived for five days. Bebb said, "UT had never known tragedy of such magnitude." Assistant coach George Cafego spoke for the staff when he said, "People get killed all over the world, and we never give it a second thought. Then it happens here at home, and it really hits you." Team captain Hal Wantland said for the players, "You just don't play for coaches, you learn to love them and respect them."

Vol players wore black crosses on their helmets against Houston the following Saturday and won 17–8, but the win could not chase away the pervasiveness of the sense of loss. Bebb said, "The victory had no real meaning in view of what had happened that week."

Maybe it was when your puppy died, your best friend moved away, a family member died, or your older sibling left home. Sometime in your youth or early adult life, you learned that loss was a part of life.

You also learned that you were virtually helpless to prevent the loss or escape it. You do have one sure place to turn, though. Jesus can share your pain and ease your suffering, but he doesn't stop there. Through the loss of his own life, he has transformed death—the ultimate loss—into the ultimate gain of eternal life.

> When the Great Scribe comes to write against
> your name, he marks not that you won or lost,
> but how you played the game.
> —LEGENDARY SPORTSWRITER GRANTLAND RICE

> *Jesus not only eases the pain of our losses but transforms the loss caused by death into the gain of eternal life.*

Getting Better

Read Hebrews 6:1–12.

"Let us go on toward perfection" (v. 1).

Many consider her the greatest player in the history of women's basketball. Once upon a time, though, she couldn't even get picked for a playground team.

Chamique Holdsclaw's legendary exploits on the basketball court include leading the Lady Vols to three straight national championships (1996–98), being named a four-time all-American, becoming the first woman ever to win the Sullivan Award as the top amateur athlete in the country, and winning a gold medal in the Olympics.

But she didn't start out that good. Randy Moore wrote in *Hoop Tales: Tennessee Lady Volunteers* that when she was about twelve, Holdsclaw discovered a basketball court near her home. The neighborhood boys played pickup games there, but they wouldn't let her play. She was a girl, and she wasn't good enough.

They were right on both counts. When Holdsclaw finally got a chance to play with the boys, she learned, as Moore said, that "she wasn't big enough, strong enough, fast enough, or skilled enough to compete with the guys." She admitted, "I was actually horrible. Nobody wanted to pick me."

That realization only made her work harder to get better. And she did get better . . . and kept getting better. Before long she was the best player on the playground, on her way to becoming the best player in the world.

Nobody's perfect; even Chamique Holdsclaw commits turnovers in the pros. But she keeps working to get better—and so do you. You attend training sessions and seminars to improve your job performance. You take golf or tennis lessons and practice to get better. You play that new video game until you master it.

To get better at anything requires a dedication, involving practice, training, study, and preparation. Improvement never comes easy. Your faith life is no different. Commit yourself to drawing closer to God, seeking perfection in that relationship knowing that you will surely find it in eternity.

Champions never complain. They are too busy getting better.
—Source unknown

▸ **You work hard to get better in all phases of your life; that should include your faith.**

Celebration Time

Read Exodus 14:26–31; 15:19–21.

"The prophet Miriam, Aaron's sister, took a tambourine in her hand; and all the women went out after her with tambourines and with dancing" (v. 15:20).

O nce upon a time, beating Vanderbilt in football was cause for a joyous and raucous celebration in Knoxville.

When the two teams met in 1914, UT was having its greatest season ever, undefeated and untied. In *The Big Orange*, Russ Bebb wrote that the game with Vanderbilt was "THE GAME of the season" and "the most talked-about and long-awaited game in Tennessee's history." The two teams had met twelve times previously, and Tennessee had managed only a 0–0 tie in 1900. Vandy had won the other eleven games, most in runaways.

But twenty years of frustration ended on November 7. Tennessee won 16–14 as Goat Carroll—a Nashville native—scored all of UT's points. He then had the team over to his home for dinner to begin celebrating the victory. Back in Knoxville, the win "created such rejoicing that classes at UT were suspended for a day of celebration." Perhaps more than a little miffed by the loss, the Vandy chancellor sniffed at all the bedlam by charging Tennessee "with over-emphasis on athletics and under-emphasis on academics."

That 1914 team gave its fans more cause for celebration by winning Tennessee's first conference championship. As Bebb noted, "The UT community was in a state of bedlam."

Invite some friends over, turn on the game on TV, fire up the grill, pull out the salsa and chips, and you've got a party. It doesn't even have to be game day; any old excuse will do. All you need is a sense that life is pretty good right now.

Jesus turns all of life into a celebration of the good life. No matter what tragedies or setbacks life may have in store, the heart given to Jesus will find the joy in living. The party never stops when a life is celebrated with Jesus!

Aim high and celebrate that!
—MARATHON RUNNER BILL RODGERS

▶ **With Jesus, life is one big party, a celebration of victory and joy.**

Basilio, Tony. "Full Circle: Former Vol Jerry Colquitt Comes Back Around." *Metro Pulse.* http:www.metropulse.com/articles/2005/15_20/sports.shtml.

Bebb, Russ. *The Big Orange: A Story of Tennessee Football.* Huntsville, AL: The Strode Publishers, 1973.

Bialik, Carl. "Forget Football: Harris, Vols Have Tennessee Buzzing about Basketball." CNN/*Sports Illustrated.* http://sportsillustrated.cnn.com/basketball/college/features/2000/spotlight/tony_harris.

Browning, Al. *Third Saturday in October: The Game-by-Game Story of the South's Most Intense Football Rivalry.* 2nd ed. Nashville: Cumberland House, 2001.

Cawood, Chris. *Legacy of the Swamp Rat: Tennessee Quarterbacks Who Just Said No to Alabama.* Kingston, TN: Magnolia Hill Press, 1994.

Cohran, Jeff. "All in the Family for Olupona." *Daily Beacon,* March 16, 2004. http://dailybeacon.utk.edu/showarticle.php?articleid=45660.

Culpepper, R. Alan. "The Gospel of Luke: Introduction, Commentary, and Reflections." Vol. IX, *The New Interpreter's Bible.* Nashville: Abingdon Press, 1998.

Fulmer, Phillip, with Jeff Hagood. *A Perfect Season,* Nashville: Rutledge Hill Press, 1999.

Gilbert, Bob. *Neyland: The Gridiron General.* Savannah: Golden Coast Publishing Co., 1990.

Gossett, Ward. *Volunteers Handbook: Stories, Stats and Stuff About Tennessee Football.* Wichita: The Wichita Eagle and Beacon Publishing Co., 1996.

Grodin, Dana Heiss. "Tennessee Pitcher Prepared for Opposing Batters, Draft." *USA Today.* http://www.usatoday.com/sports/college/baseball/2005-04-20-heiss-grodin_x.htm.

Harris, Haywood, and Gus Manning. *Six Seasons Remembered: The National Championship Years of Tennessee Football.* Knoxville: The University of Tennessee Press, 2004.

Horn, Alan. "Vol Hostess Program Changes Its Name, Policies." *Daily Beacon,* July 22, 2005. http://dailybeacon.utk.edu/showarticle.php?articleid=17274.

Klein, David. "Cross Country Preview." *Daily Beacon,* August 30, 2005. http://dailybeacon.utk.edu/showarticle.php?articleid=48288.

MacArthur, John. *Twelve Ordinary Men.* Nashville: W Publishing Group, 2002.

Moore, Randy. *Hoop Tales: Tennessee Lady Volunteers.* Guilford, CT: The Globe Pequot Press, 2005.

————. *Hoop Tales: Tennessee Volunteers Men's Basketball*. Guilford, CT: The Globe Pequot Press, 2005.

————. *Stadium Stories: Tennessee Volunteers*. Guilford, CT: The Globe Pequot Press, 2004.

Morton, Jesse. "Lady Vol Rowing Team Prepared for Season after Strenuous Summer." *Daily Beacon,* August 14, 2004. http://dailybeacon.utk/edu/showarticle.php?articleid=46886.

Parker, Barry, and Robin Hood. *Neyland: Life of a Stadium*. Chattanooga: Parker Hood Press, Inc., 2000.

Summitt, Pat, with Sally Jenkins. *Raise the Roof: The Inspiring Inside Story of the Tennessee Lady Vols' Undefeated 1997–98 Season*. New York: Broadway Books, 1998.

TheGoal.com. "Reggie White." http://www.thegoal.com/players/football/white_reggie/white_reggie.html.

University of Tennessee. "Lindsey Nelson Stadium." http://ut-sports.cstv.com/facilities/tenn-facilities-lindsey.html.

————. "Mascot: 'Smokey.'" http://utsports.cstv.com/trads/tenn-trads.html.

————. "Ron Widby Led the Vols to the SEC Title in 1966–67." http://utsports.cstv.com/sports/m-baskbl/specrel/030205aad.html.

Ward, Austin. "Johnson Looks to Replace Piantadosi." *Daily Beacon,* April 20, 2005. http://dailybeacon.utk.edu/showarticle.php ?articleid=16937.

———. "Retamoza's Success Vital to Lady Vols." *Daily Beacon,* September 21, 2004. http://dailybeacon.utk.edu/showarticle .php?articleid=47353.

Warner, Cliff. *SEC Sports Quotes.* Baton Rouge: CEW Enterprises, 2002.

West, Marvin. *Tales of the Tennessee Vols: Volunteer Legends, Landmarks, Laughs and Lies.* N.p.: Sports Publishing L.L.C., 2001.

Wikipedia. "Willie Gault." http://en.wikipedia.org/wiki/Willie_ Gault.

*Now that you've studied the playbook, these ninety winning replays
can help you stay on top of your game.*

1. Every day is not just a dawn; it is a precious chance to start over or begin anew.

2. Your attitude determines more than your mood; it shapes the kind of person you are.

3. Choose your words carefully; they are the most powerful force you have for good or for bad.

4. You have readily available a set of instructions on how to assemble your life: the Bible.

5. Prayer is powerful; it may even change God's mind.

6. No riches or luxuries must come before God in your life.

7. To follow Jesus is to act with love at all times, in all things, and toward all people.

8. For God, a joyful noise is a heartfelt "thank you," even when it's whispered.

9. Even though you keep making mistakes, God never gives up on you.

10. Renovation and sprucing up should be ongoing for your body and soul.

11. God has a job for you: spreading his love.

12. Life demands more than mere physical toughness; you must be spiritually tough too.

13. Faithfulness to God requires faith even in—especially in—the hard times.

14. Jesus is the ultimate makeover artist; he can make you over without changing the way you look.

15. Success in life takes planning and strategy; success in death does too, and God has the plan for you.

16. Jesus gives us something better than a dream; he gives us a promise.

17. You may not know it, but just like the sports stars, you have a cheerleader: God.

18. In our ever-changing and bewildering world, God is the only constant.

19. You can run to eternity by going to your knees.

20. While God controls the rain, he controls your life only if you choose to let him. Will you?

21. Life is a test that God wants you to ace.

22. It's so overused it's become a cliché, but it's true neverthe-less: Smile! God loves you.

23. You may not have a fine opinion of your body, but God thought enough of it to personally create it for you.

24. Rather than constraining you, commitment lends mean-ing to your life, releasing you to move forward with pur-pose.

25. Men and women who allow Jesus to rule their lives are anything but ordinary.

26. Our words—including profane ones—expose what's in our hearts.

27. God gives you the freedom to choose: life or death. What will you do?

28. Living in faith requires constant study and training, prepa-ration for the day when you'll meet God face-to-face.

29. God cares about all his creatures, and he expects us to re-spect them too.

30. Life is unpredictable, and tomorrow is uncertain. Only eter-nity is a sure thing—because God controls it.

31. People, things, and organizations will let you down. Only God can be trusted absolutely and confidently.

32. Fatherhood is a tough job, but a model for the father-child

relationship is found in that of Jesus the Son with God the Father.

33. Jesus understood the passion people have for fishing and commanded that it become not just a hobby but a way of life.

34. Forgiving others frees you from your past, turning you loose to get on with your life.

35. God speaks in a whisper, not a shout, so you must listen carefully or you will miss his voice altogether.

36. Being truly smart means trusting in God rather than only in your own smarts.

37. Resentment and anger over a wrong injures you, not the other person, so forget it—just as Jesus taught.

38. Pride can be dangerous because it tempts you to lower your sight from God and the eternal to the world and the temporary.

39. God chooses to keep much about himself shrouded in mystery, but one day we will see and understand.

40. God let humans kill him—and then refused to stay dead. That's amazing, but the best part is that he did it for you.

41. God will sound a final wake-up call at which even the sleepiest will arise.

42. God sent his Word—as Jesus—to make an impression on us.

43. God moves in his own time, so often we must wait, remaining faithful and hopeful.

44. Hospitality is an outward sign of the inward loving and generous nature of the host.

45. The fact of your birth made you an heir: You inherit your relatives, the world situation, and the gifts God gives you through Jesus.

46. Whatever else you give up on in your life, don't give up on God. He will never ever give up on you.

47. God's promises sound too good to be true, but the only catch is that there is no catch.

48. Jesus matter-of-factly told us what he has planned: He will return to gather all the faithful to himself.

49. Nobody can match God when it comes to giving, but you can give him the gift of your love in return.

50. Where you live may largely be the culmination of a series of circumstances; what you are is a choice you make.

51. God promises you rest that goes beyond eight hours in the sack or a day spent lounging in front of the TV.

52. The only true way to go out in style is to leave this life with praise from God.

53. God is a gentleman, soliciting your attention politely and then patiently waiting for you to give him the courtesy of a reply.

54. We all have some pretty bad ideas during our lifetimes, but nothing equals the folly of turning away from Jesus.

55. Unbridled joy can send you jumping all over the place; Jesus said such exultation should not be something rare but a way of life.

56. The awesome power of lightning pales beside God's power to control it, and yet God acts toward you with gentleness and love.

57. Jesus speaks across all language barriers because his message of hope and meaning resounds with people everywhere.

58. To be serious about Jesus is to act out of character: Rather than acting like yourself, you act like him.

59. You can never foresee what God will demand of you, but obedience requires being ready to do whatever God asks.

60. Frustration is a vexing part of life, but God expects us to handle it gracefully.

61. In the building of your life, you must start with a good, solid foundation, or the first trouble that shows up will knock you down.

62. Life seems to get ever more complicated, but God gives simple directions: Believe, trust, and obey.

63. Mamas often sacrifice for their children, but God, too, will do anything out of love for his children, including dying on a cross.

64. Physical conditioning is good, but you also need to be in peak spiritual shape.

65. In your scars lie stories. The same is true for Jesus, whose scars tell of his love for you.

66. Whether death is your worst enemy or a solicitous chauffeur is a matter of perspective.

67. An encounter with Jesus Christ sets a life on a new road to adventure.

68. You can't control the people you love, so you have a choice: Love them in spite of what they do, or drive them away.

69. For followers of Jesus, family comes not from a shared ancestry but from a shared faith.

70. Our souls thirst for the refreshing presence of God.

71. To be on God's team requires the heart of a champion.

72. Jesus expects you to do what he has told you to do—but it's because he loves you and wants the best for you.

73. Life unwinds as God wants it to, confounding us because—unlike God—we can't see the end of the story.

74. Your attitude about money says much about your attitude toward God.

75. Friends and family may help us heal up physically; Jesus tends to our spiritual healing.

76. Serving God doesn't necessarily mean entering full-time ministry and going to a foreign land; God calls you to serve him right where you are.

77. God's list is a set of instructions on how you are to conduct yourself with other people and with him.

78. We have no secrets before God; good thing he's on our side.

79. You may not get the respect you deserve, but dare to succeed anyway.

80. God does the unexpected to remind us of his presence—like showing up as Jesus.

81. God does not condemn you for being successful and enjoying popular culture, but your loyalty must lie first and foremost with him.

82. You have your own peculiar set of fears, but they need never paralyze you, because God is greater than anything you fear.

83. Making peace instead of fighting takes courage and strength, but it's certainly the less painful option.

84. The glory of this earth is fleeting, but the glory we find in Jesus lasts forever.

85. No matter how far off the beaten path you travel, you're still on holy ground, because God is there.

86. Unlike life's playing field, God's playing field is level, because everyone has equal access to what God has done through Jesus Christ.

87. God did not create you ten feet tall and bulletproof, so he arms you with his strength and his power.

88. Jesus not only eases the pain of our losses but transforms the loss caused by death into the gain of eternal life.

89. You work hard to get better in all phases of your life; that should include your faith.

90. With Jesus, life is one big party, a celebration of victory and joy.